SHANGHAI COOPERATION ORGANISATION

Shanghai Cooperation Organisation

Eurasian Security through Cooperation

L.C. Kumar

Maulana Abul Kalam Azad Institute of Asian Studies, Kolkata

SHIPRA

ISBN: 978-81-7541-580-5

First Published in India in 2010

Shanghai Cooperation Organisation:
Eurasian Security through Cooperation

Published by:
SHIPRA PUBLICATIONS
H.O.: LG 18-19, Pankaj Central Market, Patparganj,
I.P. Ext., Delhi-110092, Tel: 91-11-2223 5152, 2223 6152
Br.Off.: 4617/18, Ansari Road, Darya Ganj,
New Delhi-110002, Tel: 6594 6453, 9810522367
E-mail: info@shiprapublications.com
www.shiprapublications.com

Preface

The present study is a brief sketch outlining the origin, growth and development of the Shanghai Cooperation Organisation (SCO), the youngest of all regional security organizations in the world. The SCO covers the largest area inhabited by more than one-third of the world's population (if one were to include the population of the countries having the status of observers). The Shanghai Cooperation Organisation (SCO) can be said to have arisen out of confidence building efforts between the former USSR and the People's Republic of China which continued after the break-up of the USSR and culminated in the formation of the Shanghai Five mechanism in 1996. With the participation of Uzbekistan as the sixth member, it entered the global scene as the SCO in 2001 at its Shanghai Summit in 2001.

The organization which includes besides six permanent members, India, Mongolia, Iran and Pakistan as observers, completed eight years of its existence in 2009. As the present study brings out, the Shanghai Cooperation Organisation is marked by its openness and conformity with the principles of UN Charter and international law and reliance on regional security through non-military means by promoting regional economic cooperation. The organization is also unique insofar as it includes countries which are neighbours in and around the vast Eurasian continent.

The SCO is functioning as a regional cooperation organization trying to tackle the non-traditional threats to regional security. The organization, which in several respects appears to be overlapping with the Collective Security Treaty Organisation (CSTO) of the members of the Commonwealth of Independent States (CIS) may be perceived as a Eurasian buffer together with the CSTO, keeping at a distance the NATO which is continuously expanding eastward.

The study consists of four chapters, namely, Emergence of a Regional Security System in Eurasia: A Historical perspective; The Shanghai Five Mechanism: A Precursor to Shanghai Cooperation Organisation; The Legal and Organisational Structure of the SCO; and finally the SCO: Retrospect and Prospect.

The author has used the official documents of the Shanghai Cooperation Organisation as primary source material for this study. Works of noted Russian Specialists on the SCO as well as articles, commentaries and write-ups in the Russian, Chinese, Western and Indian press and periodicals have also been used as secondary source material.

The author would like to express his deep sense of gratitude to Prof. Devendra Kaushik, the then Chairman of the Institute, whose invaluable guidance and supervision has helped a lot in completing the project. Thanks are also due to Maulana Abul Kalam Azad Institute of Asian Studies, Kolkata for financial support for the project.

New Delhi **L.C. Kumar**

Contents

Appendices

One

Emergence of a Regional Security System in Eurasia: A Historical Perspective

The state of Sino-Soviet/Russian relations has been a vital factor in the emergence of a regional system ensuring security and cooperation on the vast Eurasian landmass comprising the territories of Russia and China and the five Central Asian states forming part of the former Soviet Union. Historically speaking, Russia and China have in general had no antagonistic or inimical relations in the past. In fact, both the Russian and Chinese people suffered as a result of the Mongol nomadic invasion led by the great conqueror of his times Chenghez Khan and his descendants against whom they waged a long struggle. Of course, the Tsarist Russian empire which grew out of the expansion of the Moscow state in the post-Mongol period did develop a clash of territorial interests with Manchu China in the present-day Maritime and Amur regions leaving behind a difficult legacy of a border problem to be resolved by the Soviet Union.

But even this problem would not have arisen if the Russian

Tsar had heeded the advice of the Russian statesman Count Sergei Witte who was an ardent votary of Eurasianism and championed the cause of good neighborly relations with China. Witte is reported to have warned the Tsar against the ill-consequences of seizing Chinese territory. The refusal of the Tsar to heed the advice of Witte led to Russia's humiliating defeat in the Russo-Japanese war of 1904-1905.[1] Witte had proposed cooperation between France, Germany and Russia for building a system of railroads connecting Europe with Asia which was subverted by British diplomacy pursuing the geopolitical game based on the ideas of Mackinder and Mahan.

It is not uncommon to come across perceptions of the Soviet-Chinese relations as basically adversarial and antagonistic because of the so-called clash of "national interests", between the two countries notwithstanding the protestations of proletarian internationalism by them. Such perceptions are, however, largely one-sided and over-simplistic. It is not fair to characterize the Sino-Soviet relations as wholly antagonistic on the basis of the Sino-Soviet ideological rift that put them to a severe strain lasting over a period of more than two decades. This led even to a brief armed conflict over an island in the Ussuri River in the late sixties. Beginning with August 1937 when the Soviet Union signed the non-aggression treaty with the Republic of China then under attack from militarist Japan pledging complete moral, political, military and technological support, Moscow made a significant material contribution to the building of modern industries and a strong military power in the post-1949 People's Republic of China. In November 1937, Stalin told the Chinese military delegation, "We shall help you regardless of how much money or material it takes".[2] The united national anti-Japanese front was always at the centre of attention of the Soviet leadership. The arms delivered to China were fairly distributed between the forces of the KMT and the CPC. Thanks to the valuable Soviet assistance China was successful in strengthening its sovereignty and re-establishing its territorial integrity. Beijing obtained international recognition as a great power and became a permanent member of the UN Security Council.

Positive Soviet Legacy for Regional Cooperation

According to Russian Sinologist, A. Lukin, the Soviet Union "left behind new independent states formed on its territory, on the whole not a bad baggage in the field of relations with China".[3] The last Soviet leader M.S. Gorbachev, writes Lukin, while clearly giving priority to normalization and development of relations with the West also simultaneously reached the conclusion that abandonment of the old conflict with China—the second strongest socialist state—after the Soviet Union would serve the interests of world socialism. He had a favourable opinion about the Chinese economic reforms which some of his advisers and experts projected as an example for the USSR to follow. Besides this, the policy of M.S. Gorbachev itself liquidated the "three big obstacles" which in the opinion of Beijing obstructed the normalization of bilateral relations between the two states. Withdrawal of Soviet troops from Afghanistan and Mongolia and ending support for the pro-Vietnam regime in Cambodia and reduction of military forces on the frontier with China were not meant as concessions to China but were organic part of the general strategy of Gorbachev's leadership. The course of improvement in relations with China was from the point of view of internal political policy not likely to be viewed as defeat; on the contrary, it could be projected as an achievement of sorts.[4] In contrast with the policy pursued by Gorbachev in relation to the West which was perceived as unilateral concession, the policy of restoration of normal relations with Beijing was for different reasons supported by all forces within the country. Thus the process of normalization of bilateral relations with China which had already been signaled during the last years of Brezhnev's rule in the early 80s of the 20th century was practically completed by 1990 with the exchange of state visits of the leaders of the two countries. In 1989 Soviet leader Gorbachev visited Beijing and was received by Deng Tsiao Ping followed by the Moscow visit of China's Prime Minister Li Peng.

The growing warmth in the bilateral relations gave an impetus to negotiations on the frontier question. In April 1990 Moscow and Beijing concludes the "Agreement on the Guiding Principles of Mutual Reduction of Armed Forces and Strengthening of Confidence in the Military Field in the Soviet-Chinese Border Region". By this agreement the two sides undertook the commitment to "implement mutual reduction of armed forces and strengthening of confidence in the military field in the border region by deciding upon concrete reduction of armed forces following negotiations.[5] In May 1991, just a few months before the disintegration of the Soviet Union, Moscow and Beijing signed the "Agreement on Soviet-Chinese State Borders in its Eastern Part" completing thereby the process of negotiations which began in 1964.[6]

The "Shanghai process" was the continuation of the Soviet-Chinese negotiations in two directions. The first direction was continuation of negotiations for concretization of confidence-building measures and practical reduction of armed forces along the borders which were now conducted jointly by Russia, the Republics of Kazakhstan, Kyrgyzstan, Tajikistan, on the one side, and China, on the other. The second direction was continuation of negotiations on borders, first of all, in its western part, which were inherited by the former Soviet Republics.

The negotiations on confidence building measures led to two agreements between the members of "the Shanghai Five": about strengthening of confidence in the military field in the border region in 1996, and mutual reduction of armed forces in the border region in 1997. In these documents the sides agreed to adopt wide measures in the border region, by partly exchanging information on the agreed components of the armed forces on the border; not to conduct any exercises aimed against the other side, and to limit exercises as a whole; reduce armed forces within a 100 km zone on both sides of the border to the level agreed upon; not to deploy on it river ships of the military naval forces; mutually invite observers for military exercises, etc.[7] The term "Shanghai five" came into vogue at the summit meeting held in Shanghai in April 1996.

However, unresolved questions of demarcation of borders continued to complicate the mutual relations of the two powers. In September 1994 Moscow and Beijing signed the agreement on Russian-Chinese state border in its western sector. By Article 6 of the Treaty signed by the heads of Russian Federation and the People's Republic of China in 2001 known as Treaty of Good-Neighbourliness, Friendship and Cooperation, the two countries for the first time in the history of their bilateral relations referred to absence of mutual territorial claims and also proclaimed their allegiance to international legal principles of inviolability of state territory and borders. The signatories of the 2001 Treaty undertook the obligation to continue the negotiations for resolving the question relating to the demarcation of the line of frontier between Russia and China in the sectors where it had not been finally demarcated in terms of the 1991 agreement, and pending that, respect the status quo. In September 2003 the Russian Deputy Foreign Minister A.P. Lasyukov answering a question from the journalists stated that there were no disputed parts of Russia-China borders and so far as two parts of the still not agreed border were concerned these constituted only 2 per cent of the entire length and that both sides were committed to finding an optimum mutually agreeable solution in these parts.[8] Soon such a solution was found. During the visit of Russian President Vladimir Putin to China in October 2004, a supplementary agreement was signed by the Foreign Ministers of the two countries on the Russia-China border in its eastern part which in the words of the Chinese leader Hu Jintao represented "the final solution of the boundary questions between the two countries".[9]

The boundary question between China and Kazakhstan was resolved by the April 1994 agreement and the supplementary agreements signed in 1997 and 1998. As President of the People's Republic of China, Jiang Zemin observed, "as a result of these agreements the two states resolved all border questions and received peaceful and friendly frontiers capable of stimulating joint prosperity".[10] In November 1999 in the Joint China-Kazakhstan communiqué the two sides affirmed full and final solution of the boundary question. In May 2002 the Foreign Ministers of China and Kazakhstan signed in Beijing a Protocol on Demarcation of Borders and announced that the signing of this Protocol signified full solution of the frontier problem in the interest of the peoples of China and Kazakhstan.[11] The boundary question between the Republic of Kyrgyzstan and China was resolved by the bilateral boundary agreement in

1996 and the supplementary agreement in 1999. In August 1999 the leaders of China, Kyrgyzstan and Kazakhstan concluded an agreement on the meeting point of the boundaries of the three countries. In the same month an agreement on Tajik-Chinese frontiers was signed. In July 2000 an agreement on the meeting point of the boundaries between China, Kyrgyzstan and Tajikistan was concluded. Thus the questions of boundaries between the former Republics of USSR and China were on the whole resolved.

Resolving the boundary question by directly continuing the trends that began while the USSR was in existence, the members of the "Shanghai Five" advanced further. Recognizing the need for further widening their cooperation, they founded the new regional organization—the Shanghai Cooperation Organization (SCO). Gradually the states of the region discovered other common interests and proceeded beyond the solution of the boundary problems to cooperation in matters of security and economic and cultural development. Uzbekistan which has no common border with China also joined the SCO which now encompassed the whole of Eurasia with the sole exception of Turkey. Afghanistan, India Pakistan and Mongolia too joined this organization with the status of observers.

A strategy of building an area of peace by firmly declining to join the US and Western Powers led military blocs was evolved jointly by India and China during the first half of the 50s of the last century. As tension began to travel from Europe to Asia in the 1952-1955 period with the creation of SEATO and the Baghdad pact, together with China, India formulated the strategy of ensuring security through cooperation based on the *Panchshila* or the Five Principles of Peaceful Co-existence embodied in the Sino-Indian agreement on Tibet in 1954.

The Panchshila approach to security relied on peaceful cooperation rather than military competition among nations for preservation of peace. The Bandung Conference of Afro-Asian states held in 1955 adopted this approach to security jointly evolved by India and China.

In the opinion of Indian scholar Devendra Kaushik, the June 1969 proposal of Soviet leader Leonid Brezhnev for a system of collective security in Asia was a continuation of the Sino-Indian joint approach of security through peaceful cooperation and not through military means. It was, however, according to Kaushik misconstrued as directed at isolating China under conditions of sharp ideological differences between the Soviet Union and China mainly related to the character of social transformation going on in the countries of the Third World and the policy of non-alignment. He cites the comments of French weekly *Le Monde* on the Brezhnev proposal on Asian security which wrote in its issue of 16 July 1969: "The system Russians envisage would be a very open one … it would not be directed against anyone and in suitable circumstances non-Asian powers might participate …. The suggestion is for a pact that would be neither anti-Chinese nor anti-American".[12] Kaushik thus views the emergence of the Shanghai Five and the SCO as "a shot in arm" for the drive towards Asian security after "a long pause" due to the Sino-Soviet rift. Yet the demise o the Soviet Union which is sometimes perceived as a causal factor in the Sino-Russian rapprochement leading to the formation of the Shanghai Cooperation Organization may have played but a marginal role. As discussed above the Sino-Soviet rift was already healing during the latter half of the 80s of the last century.

Russian-Chinese Relations: Future Prospects

Russian-Chinese relations continue to be a subject of intense debate and discussion among experts and policy-makers in both countries as well as in other states particularly the United States. While these discussions are free and frank in Russia and the West, this is not the case with China where the press and policy making institutions do not air their views publicly. In the opinion of a Russian China expert, Alexander Lukin, "Russian approaches to China differ among various groups, political trends and individual experts; moreover, they exist not in vacuum, but within the framework of more general perceptions of the international situation and Russia's position therein."[13] Lukin thus concludes: "Based on these perceptions, it can be expected that Russia will develop closer relations with China in the foreseeable future". However, he also thinks that since official Russian attitude towards China strongly depends on Russia's relations with the West, especially with the United States, US policy towards Russia and China will significantly influence the future Russian-Chinese partnership.[14]

Supporters of close friendship or alliance, with China are not confined to communists only. They may be found among non-communist nationalists and pro-Chinese liberals. Among the academics supporters of Russia's alliance with China are mainly concentrated in the Institute of the Far East of the Russian Academy of Sciences. This Institute was founded in 1966. It had many experts on China who worked under the leadership of Oleg Rakhmanin of the Central Committee of the CPSU. They provided arguments against the Maoists in the period that witnessed an acute ideological struggle against Maoist China. After the disintegration of the USSR these experts changed their views and became pro-Chinese. Among such experts a leading place was held by Alexander Yakovlev who died only recently. From an outspoken critic of the "adventurous course of foreign policy" of the heirs of Mao, Yakovlev completely reversed his position to an almost full endorsement of Beijing's foreign policy. He explained that the collapse of the Soviet Union's socialist regime left China as the principal integral part of the socialist pole in the international community. In the new situation it is only natural for Russia and China to become allies. Russia and China, possibly with India can, Yakovlev argued, "act as inspirers and organizers of a new anti-hegemonic anti-western international front."[15]

Another left-leaning publicist favouring Russia-China axis is Vsevolod Ovchinnikov who commenting on the Russian Chinese 1997 summit wrote that while Russia and China do not wish to revive the military-political alliance of the 1950s, they were being pushed in the direction of rapprochement and becoming "each other's strategic rear by the shortsighted plans of NATO's expansion to the East and turning the American-Japanese security treaty into an anti-Chinese coalition in the Far East'.[16]

The stand of the pro-Chinese non-communist nationalists which is close to that of the communist sympathizers is often more radical. Thus Alexei Mitrafanov, the Deputy Leader of the Liberal Democratic Party of Russia (LDPR) headed by V. Zhirinovsky is of the view that the confrontation between East and West would be transformed into confrontation between the continents of Eurasia and North America. To make Russia's position in this future confrontation stronger Mitrafanov proposes the formation of a "Berlin-Moscow-Tokyo" axis to be further reinforced with a Russia-China-India axis.[17]

According to A. Lukin, "Although call for a close alliance with China at present does not represent Moscow's official position, it is popular among various influential groups—traditional heavy and military industry managers and the communist faction of the Duma". This view came very close to becoming part of official policy in 1998-99 when Y. Primakov became the Foreign Minister to be elevated later to the office of Prime Minister. During his Delhi visit in December 1998 Primakov even put forth the idea of creating a Russia-China-India triangle which was immediately supported by communist leader Zyuganov. However, Beijing and Delhi were lukewarm to this proposal at that time. Nationalist and communist authors still continue to advocate an alliance with China in articles published in papers like *Zavtra* and *Sovetskaya Rossiya*.

A large group of Russian academics and politicians, however, advocate a balanced policy towards China. This position at the moment is most influential and coincides with the views usually expressed by the officials of the Foreign ministry. The writings of the Vice-Rector of the Russian Diplomatic Academy, Yevgeny Bazhanov and such leading researchers as Vilya Gel'bras of the Moscow University Institute of Asia and Africa, L. Delyusin of the Russian Academy of Sciences Institute of Oriental Studies and K.E. Sorokin of the Russian Academy of Sciences Institute of World Economy and International Politics, represent this balanced approach towards China.

The chief spokesman of the above mentioned stream of opinion believed to be closer to the official Russian approach is Bazhanov. He is critical of both—those who favour "restoration of the former military-political alliance with China" and those who go to the other extreme of "clamouring against a mounting Chinese menace". Bazhanov argues that a new Moscow-Beijing axis is both unlikely and potentially detrimental to Russian interests. He is of the view that the official Chinese line does not favour a relationship of alliance. Moreover, such an initiative on the part of Russia would further antagonize the NATO and will not be liked by most of the Asian states likely to occupy an important position in the world economy before long. It would cut off Russia from financial, commodity and technological resources and impede its plans for economic modernization and social democratization. Bazhanov is also critical of those who want that Russia should join forces with the West and advanced Asian states (Japan) against China. He does not think that China can afford a policy of expansionism in the foreseeable future as it is 'doomed' to maintaining its course of reform and cooperation with the wider world. China, according to him, is not in a position to divert its attention from its economic and social problems and get involved in expansionist drive and conflicts with other countries.[18] Another representative of the group favouring balanced relationship with China—V. Gel'bras is of the opinion that China's development poses both opportunities and challenges for Russia and rest of the world.

China is already emerging as a formidable new power in the Far East. Its economic problems and overpopulation and lack of natural resources might lead to Chinese migration. "Greater China" constitutes a potential problem for Russia in the Far East. But Gel'bras calls the fear of Chinese demographic expansion a "myth created by some politicians". He believes that if Russia approaches the Chinese challenge rationally, rapid Chinese development can provide the two countries with many opportunities for cooperation.[19]

Besides the above two trends of supporters of alliance and a balanced relationship with China, in Russia one also comes across a third trend though it is not as powerful as the former. This trend is openly opposed to close relations with China.

Among its main proponents one may mention the names of former Russian Foreign Minister Andrei Kozyrev, former Deputy Foreign Minister Georgiy Kunadze, leader of the LDPR, V. Zhirinovsky, former Prime Minister, Y. Gaidar, and Deputy Director of the Institute of the Far East, V. Myasnikov.

Kozyrev who warned President Putin against strengthening ties with China accused China of "playing the Russian card" exclusively in its own interests. He also alleged that China was Russia's "direct competitor in the struggle for attracting Western investment". Instead Kozyrev recommended developing relations with the "rich seven" western nations.[20] Kunadze wrote that while the Chinese leadership claims to reject American hegemony and possibly is even "ready to fight it ... to the last Russian", in its real policy it is too cautious and realistic to openly challenge the US, demanding equal rights.[21] Myasnikov sees China as a threat. He talks of uncontrolled mass Chinese immigration to Russia and alleges that the Chinese have already "created a well-established illegal network on the Russian territory". According to him the Chinese have coined a term "the Great Northern Virgin Land" and this theme of "Virgin Land" is being actively propagated in China.

The DPR leader V. Zhirinovsky is also a proponent of this point of view and believes that Russia has "two adversaries—the USA and China who want to destroy us". The provincial leaders in some border regions, especially the Maritime Krai and the Khabarovski Krai constitute a pressure group which lobbies against unrestricted Russian-Chinese border trade. They favour a strictly controlled border and tough measures against Chinese immigration. During the period of Yeltsin's rule the regional governors were able to take unilateral measures such as change the border control regime. Their vigorous anti-immigration propaganda resulted in an atmosphere not conducive for developing relations with China.

The centralization measures taken under president Putin have changed this situation in the regions. Now few Governors dare to challenge the official line publicly. The central leadership is also paying more attention to the needs of the Russian Far East. Addressing the conference on the development of the Russian Far East and the Trans-Baikal region held at Blagoveshchensk in June 2000 President Putin acknowledged the failure of Moscow's previous attempts to step up regional development and urged to look at the region from a global perspective. As opposed to some nationalist circles the Kremlin tends to think that the dangers facing the Russian Far East arise from problems of domestic development and not from a Chinese plot to take advantage of Russia's weaknesses. President Putin struck a note of warning to his compatriots when he said, "I do not want to dramatize the situation, but if we do not make every real effort, even the indigenous Russian population will soon speak mostly Japanese, Chinese and Korean".[22]

During his state visit to Beijing in July 2000, reinforcing a balanced approach President Putin stated that Russia should "lean on two wings: European and Asian". He further explained the Russian stand thus: "We know that Russia is both a European and Asian country. We do justice to both European pragmatism and oriental wisdom. Therefore Russia's policy should be balanced. In this sense, relations with the People's Republic of China should undoubtedly be one of our major priorities."[23] Earlier speaking at the Shanghai-Five meeting in Dushanbe the Russian President stated, "China is for us really a strategic partner in all spheres of activity".[24] In April 2001 at a meeting with the Chinese Foreign Minister Tang Jiaxuan,

Putin stated, "We practically have no problems that irritate our relations. On the contrary, relations between the two countries are developing dynamically and positively."[25]

However, the magnitude of the challenge posed by the new imperial course of the US policy to peace, security and development of the world appears to have not been taken seriously enough by the great powers which are still in a position to rebuff it by their joint efforts, not necessarily through military means. The Russian policy lacks coherence and remains ambivalent in spite of occasional expressions of support for the Eurasian direction. President Putin's address in May 2005 to the Federal Assembly is a case in point. Putin spoke about "300 years of Russia's aspirations of western style liberal democracy." He also declared Russia's determination to be a "European" power pursuing "civilizing mission" in Eurasia.[26] China is also not far behind in its vacillating course of foreign policy which remains predominantly pre-occupied with protecting its trade interests without seriously considering the alternative of forging an Asian response to the growing threat to global security from the emergence of neo-Fascist thinking in the American ruling circles.

Nevertheless, ad hocism and pragmatism at times bordering upon opportunism notwithstanding, the shared concern among Russia and China about growing US unilateralism undermining the international order rendering both international law and the UN organization redundant and ineffective has impelled them to draw closer to each other. The US policy under President Bush aimed at creation of a centre of international decision-making outside the UN without the participation of Moscow and Beijing brought them to working jointly for a multilateral world. Yet it would be wrong to perceive their willingness to work together for the cause of achieving a multipolar world as an anti-American alliance. Both the powers are still keen to seek cooperation of the United States which they consider vital for their economic reforms and modernization.

In the United States the policy-making circles are not unduly perturbed over the growing trend of Russia-China cooperation. Interestingly the RAND Corporation Report "The United States and a Rising China: Strategic and Military Implications" (1999) mentions Russia only in connection with acquisition by China of Russian arms and does not at all take any notice of the wider context of existing Russian-Chinese relations and their future development. The authors of this report also comment that China was not really interested in the formation of a multipolar world order. The Chinese emphasize the necessity of a multipolar world order only when tensions mount in Chinese-American relations, otherwise the Chinese quite happily prefer to concentrate on improving those relations rather than stress the need to curb American hegemony. Hence while opposing American hegemonism, Beijing might actually prefer its replacement not so much by a multipolar world, but sooner by a sort of a Chinese-American condominium.[27] The authors recommended the policy of containment-cum-engagement—"congagement"—towards China.

The advocates of a "balanced" policy in Russia and a "pragmatic" policy in China who are in their heart of hearts pro-West and pro-America, base their argument or the need of both Russia and China for good relations with the US and the West in order to develop their economies. They do not reject out of hand a situation when "problems with the US outweigh incentives for cooperation". They, however, pin their hopes upon the real world situation compelling the United States to correct its policies by "coming to terms with other countries, accepting that all players in the post-cold war era will have to make some concessions and compromises". Their problem is that they do not view the present US new imperial course as an outcome of a global financial and economic crisis. The more this crisis deepens the more bellicose preemptive policies are likely to be pursued by the United States. This has already landed the world in a situation of grave threat to peace and security leaving little room for "balanced" and "pragmatic" policies on the part of Russia and China. Both Moscow and Beijing may be compelled to pick up the challenge to peace in Eurasia before long and transform the Shanghai Cooperation Organization into an effective instrument to promote security and cooperation on the vast Eurasian landmass. By successfully undertaking mega projects of development of infrastructure in the field of transport and energy Russia and China along with the Central Asian Republics can help salvage the global economy on the verge of a depression.

As dissatisfaction with the US aggressive policy grows it is only natural to expect that Russia and China will gradually come closer to each other. Their cooperation is also likely to grow to cope with the new non-traditional threats to security in the region such as traffic in drug and illicit arms, illegal migration and rehabilitation of refugees. The growing differences in the Western and Sino-Russian perceptions of terrorism are also bound to result in the development of a regional mechanism to counter this threat with the joint efforts of the states in the area—Russia, China and the Central Asian Republics. The continuation of the US air bases and military presence in Central Asia even after the end of the US-led first phase of military operation in Afghanistan alarmed Russia, China and other Central Asian Republics which are members of the Shanghai Cooperation Organization. The threat of regime change in the Central Asian Republics under the guise of "colour revolutions" resulted in the SCO members forging a joint front to meet this new threat to their state sovereignty. The situation has of late apparently changed for the better with the Obama Administration's policy of engaging Russia in a constructive dialogue on global security. The new American Administration has also taken initiative to address the Russian concerns on expansion of NATO to include Ukraine and Georgia and on missile defence system in East Europe.

NOTES

1. See Devendra Kaushik, "India-Russia-China, Triangle to Transform the Present World Order" in *Asia Annual 2004*, Shipra Publications, Delhi, p. 36.
2. A.M. Ledovsky, R.A. Mirovitskaya and V.S. Mianikov, *China's Statehood and Soviet Policy in China. The Pacific War Years: 1941-1945*, Moscow, 1999. p. 46.
3. Alexander Lukin, "Shanghaiskaya Organizatsia Sotrudni-chestvo: Strukturnoe Oformlenia i perspektivy razvitiya", *Analyticheskie Zapiski*, vyp;. 2(4) Feb. 2005, p. 6.
4. *Ibid.*
5. *Sbornik Rossiisko-Kitaiskikh dogovorov*, 1949-1999, Moscow, 1999, p. 81.
6. *Ibid.*, pp. 117-25.
7. *Ibid.*, pp. 365-92.
8. A. Lukin, *op. cit.*, p. 8.
9. *Ibid.*
10. *Renmin Jibao*, 5 July 1998.
11. A. Lukin, *op. cit.*, p. 8.
12. Devendra Kaushik, "Building a New Asian Security System through Regional Cooperation: Renewal of Bandung Spirit" in Mahavir Singh (ed.), *Building a New Asia*, Shipra Publications, Delhi, 2005, p. 5.
13. Alexander Lukin, *Russia's Image of China and Russian-Chinese Relations*, p. 1, *http://pubs* Carnegie.ru/English/books/1999/04dt/default/asp?n=04 introduction asp
14. *Ibid.*
15. For a vigorous plea for a Russia-China-India Strategic Triangle, see A. Yakovlev's article "Together We Stand" in Mahavir Singh and V. Krashchilshikov (eds.); also see, A. Yakovlev, "Confidential

Partnership Aimed at Strategic Interaction" in *Far Eastern Affairs*, no. 2(112), 1997, p. 45.

16. Vsevolod Ovchinnikov, "Rossiya i Kitaya: mnogopolyarny mir, spravedlivy mezhdunarodny poryadok" in *Rossiskaya* Gazeta, 26 March 1997.
17. Alexei Mitrafanov, "Anti-NATO Novaya ideya rossiskoi geopolitiki Taktika i strategiya na sovremennom etape, unpublished manuscript, pp. 21-24 (cited by A. Lukin, *op. cit.*, p. 4)
18. Y. Bazhanov, "Big Neighbour – Big Headaches", *New Times*, August 1996, p. 47.
19. V. Gel'bras, Aziatsko-Tikhookeanskiy region: Problemy ekonomicheskoi bezopasnosti Rossiy, Moscow, 1995, p. 4. Also, *KNR Posle Den Syaopina: problemy ekonomicheskogo razvitiya.*
20. A. Kozyrev, "Riski svoi I chuzhie" *Moskovskie Novosti*, no. 30, 1 August 2000.
21. G. Kunadze, "Sindrome Kuzkinoi matery", *Novoe Vremya*, no. 37, 19 September 1999.
22. http://www.president.kremlin.ru/events/50html.
23. http://www.president.kremlin.ru/events/45html.
24. Quoted by Igor Ivanov, "Nashi vzaimootnosheniya svobodny ot emotsiy", *Rossiskaya Federatsiya* no. 10, (155) July 2000, p. 3.
25. http://www.ortv.ru.
26. *Ibid.*
27. Z. Khalllilzad, A.N. Shulsky, D. Byman, R. Cliff, D. Orletsky, D.A. Shtapak, A.J. Tellis, *The United States and a Rising China; Strategic and Military Implications*, RAND 1999, XXIII, pp. 11012.

Two

The Shanghai Five Mechanism: A Precursor to Shanghai Cooperation Organisation

It is more than a decade since the cold war came to an end in 1991 following the dissolution of the Soviet Union which typified the rival pole in the bipolar international system. Now in retrospect one is amused at the alarmist predictions made by many Europhile analysts about the continent of Asia becoming the main source of threats to global security. There was no dearth of experts forecasting acute arms race and power rivalries leading to major conflicts in Asia in the post cold war period. However, the dismal scenario arising from the aggressive actions of an expansionist China, militarized Japan and over-ambitious India has come to naught. Contrary to their apprehensions there has not been any major war in Asia since 1978-79 Vietnam, Cambodia-China conflict. The on-going Israel and Palestine conflict and India-Pakistan standoff on the Kashmir question are largely due to outside powers' encouragement. The bloody conflict in Iraq is the direct outcome of new imperialist course of unilateralism followed by the sole superpower, the USA. Similarly, the threats to peace in Asia—in Taiwan and the Korean peninsula have also a close link with Washington's policy of "defence through pre-emptive action" bypassing the United Nations.

David C. Kang has rightly observed that the "non-balancing" of Asian states against China, the lack of Japanese rearmament, and five decades of "non-invasion' by North Korea has amply proved the ability of Asian states to respond quickly to changing circumstances.[1]

Asia, comprising China, India, Japan and a large part of Russia with half of the world's population, has not been a centre of gravity in international politics until recently. Only during the last two decades this continent has emerged as a new centre of economic and military power, overtaking Europe. The most notable feature of development in Asia has been absence of inter-state war. The transformation of China into a global power has surprisingly not evoked tension among the Asian states. This has sled many observers to speak of the Asian traditions of international relations as different from the western traditions. A prosperous and strong China instead of evoking fear among Asian states has become a sheet anchor of regional stability. Beijing has resolved its territorial disputes with Afghanistan, Burma, Kyrgyzstan, Tajikistan, Mongolia, Nepal, Russia and Pakistan. It has settled its border problem with Cambodia and Vietnam and has reached an understanding with India on key principles guiding the settlement of the border problems. Of course there has remained the problem of Taiwan, and the Senkaku Island with Japan and the problem over the Spartly Island in the ASEAN region not to mention the still unresolved disputes over territories between Russia and Japan as also over an island between Japan and South Korea. But the significant thing is that no war over territory has been waged in

Asia over the last two decades. Notwithstanding continuing power rivalry between Japan and China, there is a flourishing trade between these two countries. Taiwan has invested $ 50 billion in mainland China.[2] Despite the still unresolved border problem, trade between India and China has also reached a high level. China is Japan's second largest trading partner, and between China and Vietnam, there is a high level of trade. Sino-Soviet rift has given way to Sino-Russian economic and military cooperation between the two neighbouring countries which is successfully developing to a new height. The long-standing territorial dispute between them has also been resolved to their mutual satisfaction.

Emergence of the Shanghai Five in the Panchsheel and the Bandung Spirit

As stated in the preceding chapter at a time when tensions from Europe were being transported to Asia during 1952-55 period through the Western project of a Middle East Command, the Northern Tier Strategy, the US military assistance to Pakistan, the creation of SEATO and the Baghdad pact, India under the leadership of Jawaharlal Nehru tried to meet this challenge by evolving the concept of "peace Area'. Against the Dullesian strategy of collective security through military pacts, Nehru came out with the concept of collective peace which was a further elaboration of his "area of peace concept".[3]

India jointly with China enunciated the strategy of achieving security through cooperation based on the Panchsheel or the five principles of co-existence embodied in the Sino-Indian agreement on Tibet in 1954. The Panchsheel approach to security laid stress on peaceful co-existence as against military competition among nations for preservation of peace. It aimed at creating a structure of peace in Asia based on mutual assurance by the states to conduct their relations on the basis of mutual respect for sovereignty and territorial integrity, non-interference in internal affairs, settlement of disputes through peaceful means and mutually beneficial cooperation. The 1955 Bandung conference of Afro-Asian states put its seal of approval on their approach to security evolved earlier by India and China.

After a long interval the idea of Asian security got revived with the emergence of the Shanghai Cooperation Organization. This process actually started in 1989 with negotiations on confidence building measures on the Soviet-Chinese border to help the talks already going on between the two countries to settle their border problems. These negotiations were later converted into talks on Confidence-Building Measures and Reduction of Armed Forces between China and four former Soviet republics—Russia, Kazakhstan, Kyrgyzstan and Tajikistan in the wake of disintegration of the Soviet Union. Thus the bilateral talks which started in 1989 between USSR and PRC proliferated in 1993 into multilateral negotiations between Russia, China and three Central Asian states. On 26 April 1996 the Presidents of these five states met at Shanghai to conclude 14 agreements on border confidence building measures and reduction of armed forces deployed in the border regions. Thus was born the Shanghai Five which got a new name of Shanghai Forum after Uzbekistan joined it as an observer in July 2000 at its Dushanbe summit. By now it had grown into a Eurasian regional organization to meet the challenges of normalization of relations in this region.

The Shanghai Five name was coined after the first summit of the Five states bordering Eurasia met in Shanghai in 1996 to sign "Agreements on Strengthening Military Confidence-Building Measures in Bordering Areas." The second meeting of the three Central Asian states, Russia and China took place in Moscow in 1997 when they concluded an "Agreement on Mutual Reduction of Armed forces" in border areas. The agreements signed at Shanghai and Moscow affirmed that "the military forces deployed in the border areas would remain defence-oriented and the countries confirmed they would not use "force against each other" and that "no party to the agreement seeks unilateral military security."

The agreements signed in 1996 and 1997 manifested the desire of the Shanghai Five powers to solve regional territorial disputes in a peaceful manner without third party mediation. With the border disputes among the five states resolved to a great extent they initiated discussions concerning other urgent problems facing them in the aftermath of the collapse of the Soviet Union.

The third summit of Shanghai Five met in Almaty in 1998. It took note of the situation prevailing in Central Asia following the Taliban takeover of power in Kabul. The joint statement adopted at the Almaty summit of the Shanghai Five declared that "any form of national separatism, ethnic separatism and religious extremism is unacceptable". Regarding Afghanistan, it observed "greater efforts should be made to promote a peaceful settlement of the conflict under the auspices of the UN and with the participation of the concerned countries". It also recommended that the "interests of all the national and regional groups and political forces involved in the conflict should receive due consideration".

At the next summit held at Bishkek in August 1999 an agreement was reached on practical measures for elimination of religious militancy in the region. It was the natural result of expansion of religious extremism and terrorism into Central Asia and Russia as also in the Chinese province bordering

Central Asia-Xinjiang. The member countries agreed to extend their cooperation in the field of security and also to deepening their military cooperation. All the participating countries pointed out that "to effectively crack down on international terrorism, illegal dealings in drug and narcotics trafficking, arms smuggling, illegal immigration and other forms of cross-border crimes is of significance .... The responsible departments of the five countries will adopt measures to launch practical cooperation including the consultation and working out of a programme of joint action during the period 1999-2000 .... They pledged that they would not allow anyone to use their territories to engage in actions harmful to the sovereignty, security or social order of any of the five countries". All the parties agreed to launch multilateral cooperation in economic field. They also decided to give utmost priority to the Almaty Joint Statement of 1998. The member countries agreed to set-up a joint consultative group to prepare relevant proposals for accelerating economic development.[4]

The Heads of the law enforcement agencies of Shanghai Five met in Bishkek in December 1999 as a follow-up of the Bishkek summit. The participants agreed that the law enforcement agencies of the Shanghai Five countries would apply forms and methods of cooperation including joint-operation. To execute joint operations they decided to set up the so-called Bishkek group consisting of the chiefs of the law enforcement agencies which were to meet annually.[5]

At the Dushanbe summit in 2000 which was attended by President Putin and also President Islam Karimov as observer it was decided to broaden the scope of the organization to cover diplomatic, economic, military and technological fields for strengthening regional security and stability. The leaders committed themselves to cooperation in combating traffic in narcotics and small arms and in fighting terrorism, religious extremism and separatism and also in resolving disputes over trans-border resources like water, energy and infrastructure. All the five presidents appreciated the development of the "Shanghai Five" summit process. Starting as a forum aimed at reducing hostility along the borders, the mechanism has turned out to be a new instrument for regional cooperation in political, security, law enforcement, and economic sphere. Economic and trade cooperation dominated the proceedings of the meeting. The participating Heads of States briefed the summit on the economic situation in their respective countries and presented specific projects open to other countries. While condemning the terrorist activities in the region, the Dushanbe summit promised to enhance cooperation among security and law enforcement departments. The Shanghai Rive countries agreed to support each other in efforts to preserve national sovereignty, independence, territorial integrity and social stability. The Dushanbe meeting in fact marked the conclusion of the first round of the "Shanghai Five" summit. It was held in the aftermath of the Tashkent explosions and armed incursions of militant groups in the southern region of Kyrgyzstan for taking hostages.

The June 2001 summit held in Shanghai decided to rename the Shanghai Five as Shanghai Cooperation Organization consisting of six states including Uzbekistan. The Joint Declaration issued after the summit took stock of five years of existence of the Shanghai Five, appreciating its role in promoting and deepening good neighbourliness, mutual confidence and friendship among the member countries apart from strengthening stability and security in the region. The participant countries also expressed their desire to develop a common approach towards global problems and with regard to security and economic development of the region. The summit also emphasized mutually beneficial cooperation among the participating countries in trade and economic field and efforts to promote cooperation in diverse forms on both bilateral and multilateral basis. It also underlined the need to strengthen the mechanism of consultation and coordination of their actions on regional issues. The declaration also emphasized that the SCO remains committed to the objectives and principles of mutual respect for independence, sovereignty and territorial integrity, equality and mutual benefit, solution of all issues through mutual consultations, non interference in the internal affairs, non-use of military force or threat of force and renunciation of military superiority in the adjoining areas.[6]

The heads of states agreed that the foreign and defence ministers of the SCO member countries will hold annual meetings to strengthen and expand their cooperation on major international and regional issues, first and foremost on issues concerning security and stability in Central Asia. They held that measures must be taken for speeding up the process of negotiation and signing of relevant documents to facilitate the establishment and effective operation of an anti-terrorist organization in Bishkek. The heads of states also called for the preparation of other anti-crime documents for consideration at the routine meeting of law enforcement and security officials in Kazakhstan.[7]

Thus beginning with an initiative towards confidence building measures in the border region of the five states including the two great powers, Russia and China, and the three Central Asian republics, the nascent regional mechanism of the Shanghai Five achieved considerable success in a short period of time. The spirit which led to the upgrading of the

Shanghai Five launched in 1996 into a full-fledged regional security organization was the awareness that regional security can best be realized through the sincere efforts of a group of neighbouring states in a region which consider their relationship as essentially complementary rather than adversial. The security issues including environmental protection, water management and cooperation and development of energy and transport, besides prevention of trafficking in drugs, arms and illegal migration, are best dealt through the cooperation of the states in the region themselves rather than through a security structure located outside the regions.[8] The criticism of the SCO by western analysts like Stephen Blank that the organization has been a failure as a "security provider"[9] with a long line of abortive attempts to reorganize Central Asia under Russian leadership, is unjustifiable.

It is not fair to say that the SCO has played no role in the fight against terrorism in Afghanistan and Central Asia. In fact in August 1999 at the first summit of the Shanghai Five held in Bishkek it was decided at the Russian suggestion to hold regular meetings of the heads of law enforcement agencies and Special Forces besides ministers of defence and foreign affairs. In November 2000 the representatives of the five member states held in Moscow special consultation on the situation in Afghanistan. As Russian scholar Alexander Lukin rightly points out, "Two years earlier to the terrorist attack in New York, the Shanghai Five had started working on the Convention on Struggle Against Terrorism, Separatism and Extremism which was adopted in June 2001 at the Shanghai Five summit held in the city of Shanghai. This convention reached an agreement over the definition of terrorism which has been a subject of debate (the Chechen separatists and the Palestinian suicide bombers are not accepted by some as terrorists but freedom fighters). The SCO also took concrete steps to raise anti-terrorist structures".[10]

The Shanghai Summit of the Shanghai Five powers and Uzbekistan held in June 2001 which adopted the declaration on the establishment of Shanghai Cooperation Organization also approved the Shanghai Convention on Combating Terrorism, separatism and Extremism. This convention which was a significant act of the just founded organization now appears in retrospect a historic step taken by Eurasian powers launching an effective struggle against the three evils of terrorism, extremism and separatism. Adopted less than two months before the 9/11 incident this convention is really a document of historic importance. Rejecting all hypocrisy and double standards the convention categorically declared "Terrorism, separatism, extremism" as a "threat to international peace and security". It further stated that regardless of their motives they cannot be justified under any circumstances and the perpetrators of such acts should be prosecuted under the law. Besides accepting the meaning of terrorism as an offence recognized in any of the treaties listed in the annexure of the convention, it extended the scope of terrorism to "other acts intended to cause death or serious bodily injuries to a civilian, or any other person not taking an active part in the hostilities in a situation of armed conflicts or to cause major damage to any material facility, as well as to organize, plan, aid and abet such act, when the purpose of such act, by its very nature or context, is to intimidate a population, violate public security or compel public authorities or an international organization to do or to abstain from doing any act ...". As the Declaration on Establishment of SCO recalled, "The founding and development of "Shanghai Five" conformed to the post Cold War historic trend that mankind aspires to peace and development wherein unity and cooperation can be realized through mutual respect and confidence by countries having diverse civilizational backgrounds and cultures".[11]

The Declaration affirmed that the new organization was arising "against a background of rapid development of the process of multipolarisation and information globalization in the 21st century which is conducive to the member states making use of the opportunities and responding to the new challenges and threats". The declaration also stated that SCO "adheres to the principles of non-alignment, does not target any other country or region, and is open to outside powers".[12]

The Shanghai Convention bound the parties to hold consultation, exchange views and coordinate their positions on the pertinent issues of combating acts referred to in article 1 of the Convention on struggle against terrorism, extremism and separatism. Article 6 enjoins upon the parties to assist and cooperate with each other through exchange of information, execution of request concerning operational search actions, implementation of agreed measures to prevent, identify and suppress acts referred to in Article 1 clause 1 of the convention, prevent identify and suppress financing, supplies of weapons and ammunitions or any other information concerning their practical implementation, exchange of experience in the field of prevention, suppression of acts covered by the Convention, various forms of training or re-training or upgrading of their experts and conclusion of agreements and other cooperation.[13]

The joint declaration of war on Terrorism and Religious Extremism by the six SCO states has undoubtedly made its contribution to the development of an atmosphere necessary to ensure success of the fight against international terrorism in Afghanistan and Central Asia. The SCO has not only contributed to creation of an atmosphere for unleashing an effective struggle against terrorism in Central Asia, it has also made a concrete contribution to this struggle by holding in 2004 the Sino-Kyrgyz Joint anti-Terrorist exercises and joint military manoeuvres in Kazakhstan in August 2005 with the participation of five members of the organization following the Shanghai Convention of 2001.

The SCO summit of 2002 witnessed an important advance in the setting-up of a firm legal basis for a Eurasian regional security and cooperation organization when the SCO summit adopted the Charter of the SCO and Declaration of Heads of States of the Members of the SCO. The fact that this step was taken in the wake of Russo-American agreement in Moscow for reduction of nuclear arms and the Rome Declaration establishing the Russia-NATO Joint Council has caused some misgivings about Russia's pro-US tilt. However, President Putin during his meeting with President Bush in St. Petersburg hastened to underscore the important role of the SCO.[14]

This was again emphasized by President Putin in the press conference after talks with the President of Finland when he reiterated that Russia continues to have "major interest in the East' and China was one of "Russia's critical partners". While continuing a permanent dialogue with the United States over a new global security system, Putin has also come out with the concept of a "stable arc" aimed at creation of a "buffer zone" along the NATO in the West, Collective Security Treaty Organization (CSTO) of the CIS in the middle, and the SCO in the East, with Russia as member of both the organizations. On the eve of St. Petersburg summit the Russian media highlighted a complementary multi-directional policy followed by Russia towards the United States, Europe, China and Central Asia to deal with the current challenges. Viewed in this perspective it will be improper to treat SCO as "NATO of the

East'—an alliance of Russia, China and Central Asian states to checkmate American influence in Central Asia.[15]

Chinese scholar Lu-Zhong-Wei characterizes the "Shanghai Spirit" as five "Cs" of "confidence, communication, cooperation, co-existence and common interest'. The Shanghai Spirit has shown to the world community that a system of regional security can be created on the basis of cooperation (not military competition) resulting in a "win-win" situation for all. It has also put an end to military confrontation on the Eurasian borders that lasted for over three decades. The destabilizing effect of the foreign inspired Islamist threats to territorial integrity of Russia in its northern Caucasus region and the fear of spill-over effect of growing radicalization of Islam in Central Asia has brought both China and Russia close to each other. This has resulted in their joint declaration together with the Central Asian republics to forge a regional mechanism for ensuring security through cooperation for achieving development and stabilizing peace. The American military presence in the wake of the 9/11 incidents in an area forming the "soft-underbelly" of Russia and close to the Chinese border also provided an additional impetus to the rise of the Shanghai Cooperation Organization. One cannot but agree with the conclusion of Indian scholar Devendra Kaushik:

"Notwithstanding the multiplicity of factors and their transitory nature, making possible the emergence of this organization, it cannot be denied that for the first time a new mechanism for ensuring security through peaceful cooperation has been ushered... regardless of the diverse motives of the states joining this organization. A positive development has taken place contrary to hitherto widely prevalent approach of reliance on exclusively military alliances. The uniqueness of SCO lies in its openness and all inclusive character.[16]

NOTES

1. David C. Kang, "Getting Asia Wrong", *International Security*, Vol. 27, no. 4, Spring 2003, pp. 59-85.
2. David Krager and Ichiko Fuyuno, "Innovate or Die: Reinventing Japan", *Far Eastern Economic Review*, 25 April 2002.
3. See, Devendra Kaushik and S. Preethum, *Towards Collective Security in Asia*, Delhi, 1973.
4. "Bishkek Statement", *Beijing Review*, 13 September 1999.
5. "Police, Security Chiefs of Shanghai Five States Sign Memorandum" *Interfax News Agency*, 2 Dec., 1999.
6. "Declaration of the Shanghai Cooperation Organisation", Shanghai, 15 June 2001, *China Report*, no. 37, 2001, pp. 553-56. http://www/News/Sinhuanet.com/English/2003-2005/27/Content_889169.htm
7. *People's Daily*, 15 June 2001.
8. Devendra Kaushik in *Asia Annual*, 2004, *op. cit.*
9. Stephen Blank, "The Shanghai Cooperation Organisation: A Post Mortem", *Nordic Newsletter of Asian Studies*, no. 3, 2002.
10. Alexander Lukin, *Analiticheskie Zapiski*, vyp. 2(4), February 2005, p. 10.
11. "Shanghai Convention on Combating Terrorism, Separatism and Extremism", http://www.sectsco.org/news_detail.asp?id=93&LanguageID=2
12. Declaration on Establishment of Shanghai Cooperation Organisation", http://www.sectsco.org/news_detail.asp?id= 101&LanguageID=2
13. *Ibid.*
14. Devendra Kaushik in *Asia Annual*, 2004, *op. cit.*
15. Devendra Kaushik in *Asia Annual*, 2004, *op. cit.*
16. Devendra Kaushik's unpublished Paper on Shanghai Cooperation Organisation presented at International Conference on Shanghai Cooperation Organisation in Uralsk, Kazakhstan in June 2004.

Three

The Legal and Organizational Structure of the Shanghai Cooperation Organisation

As discussed above in the previous chapter the Shanghai process which was a continuation of the Soviet-Chinese bilateral negotiations in the twin direction of concretization of Confidence Building Measures and practical reduction of conflict along the borders and settlement of border disputes between the two sides finally culminated in the setting up of the Shanghai Cooperation Organization in Shanghai on 15 June 2001 with the addition of Uzbekistan as the sixth member. The inclusion of Uzbekistan which had no common border with China signaled the extension of Shanghai Five's interest beyond the problems related to the old legacy of border disputes.

The new organization—SCO—has been since its very inception deeply interested in stabilization of the situation in Afghanistan and liquidation of religion-based terrorism in that country which created a serious threat to Uzbekistan. The Afghanistan-based terrorist organization-Taliban-actively supported the creation of a theocratic state in Uzbekistan. In February 1999 the Islamic movement of Uzbekistan organized a series of bomb blasts in Uzbekistan's capital Tashkent and made an unsuccessful attempt on the life of President Karimov. Earlier in 1998 they had created trouble in the Southern region of Kyrgyzstan. In August 2000 a large number of Islamists trained in Afghanistan had penetrated the southern region of Kyrgyzstan and from there Uzbekistan. But the Uzbek and Kyrgyz government forces expelled them. This development also helped the transformation of the Shanghai Five into the Shanghai Cooperation Organisation. Besides the three Central Asian states, China was also threatened with the rise of militant Islam in its province of Xinjiang. According to official Chinese data, from 1990 to 2001, the Islamist militants committed more than 200 terrorist acts in the different region of Xinjiang resulting in the death of six hundred persons including members of security forces.[1]

At the summit of the SCO held in St. Petersburg on 7 June 2002 the Charter of the organization was adopted. This Charter is the basic document which lays down the aims, objectives and principles of the organization as also its structure and basic direction of its activities. The Charter lays down the aims of the SCO as under:

1. Strengthening of mutual trust, friendship and good neighbourliness among the member states;
2. development of multi-vectoral cooperation with the aims of supporting and strengthening peace, security and stability of the region; assistance in construction of new democratic, just and rational political and economic international order;
3. joint struggle against terrorism, separatism and extremism in all their manifestations;

4. struggle against illegal trafficking of arms, drugs and other forms of transnational criminal activities;
5. encouragement to effective regional cooperation in political, trade and economic and defence, law enforcement, protection of environment, cultural, scientific, technical, educational, energy, transportation, credit and financial and other spheres of common interest;
6. assistance for all-round and balanced economic growth, social and cultural development in the region;
7. co-ordination of approaches towards integration into the global economy;
8. support and development of relations with other states and international organizations;
9. Cooperation for prevention of international conflicts and their peaceful resolutions;
10. Joint search for solution of problems which might arise in the 21st century;
11. Promotion of human rights and fundamental freedoms in accordance with the international obligations of the member states and their national legislation.[2]

The basic principles of the SCO are mutual respect for sovereignty and equal rights of all member states, openness and non-targeting of other regions and countries by the SCO member states. It is worth while to mention here the fact that the declaration underscored and "particular significance" of the need to preserve "global strategic balance and stability" in the current international situation. The main principles of the organization are also inserted in Article-2 of the Charter. It says:

- equality of all member States, search of common positions on the basis of mutual understanding and respect for opinions of each of them;

- gradual implementation of joint activities in the spheres of mutual interest;
- peaceful settlement of disputes between the member States
- SCO being not directed against other States and international organizations;
- prevention of any illegitimate acts directed against the SCO interests;
- implementation of obligations arising out of the present Charter and other documents adopted within the framework of SCO in good faith.
- maintenance of peace and enhancing security and confidence in the region;
- search of common positions on foreign policy issues of mutual interest, including issues arising within international organizations and international fora;
- development and implementation of measures aimed at jointly counteracting terrorism, separatism and extremism, illicit narcotics and arms trafficking and other types of criminal activity of a transnational character, and also illegal migration;
- coordination of efforts in the field of disarmament and arms control;
- support for, and promotion of regional economic cooperation in various forms, fostering favourable environment for trade and investments with a view to gradually achieving free flow of goods, capital, services and technologies;
- effective use of available transportation and communication infrastructure, improvement of transit capabilities of member States and development of energy systems;

- Sound environmental management, including water resources management in the region, and implementation of particular joint environmental programmes and projects;
- Mutual assistance in preventing natural and man-made disasters and elimination of their implications;
- Exchange of legal information in the interests of development of cooperation within SCO;
- Development of interaction in such spheres as science and technology, education, health care, culture, sports and tourism.[3]

All decisions of the SCO are to be taken by consensus with the exception of questions relating to suspension and termination of the membership of the organization. In the meeting of the heads of states of SCO held in May 2003 at Moscow the organizational formation of SCO was practically completed. Documents relating to the procedure to be followed in the activities of the statutory organs of the SCO, the emblem and the flag of the organization were finalized. The appointment of the first Executive Secretary was confirmed in this meeting. A well-known Chinese diplomat, former Deputy Foreign Minister of PRC Zhang Deguang was appointed as the Executive Secretary of the organization. The meeting also adopted an agreement on the formation and execution of the budget of the SCO. At the end of September 2003 the second meeting of the Heads of government (Prime Minister) of the member states of the SCO was held in Beijing. The budget of the organization for the year 2004 was also adopted in this meeting. The meeting also confirmed the rules for conducting the finances and remuneration and allowances to be paid to the staff members of permanent functioning of the Regional Anti-Terrorist

Structure (RATS). After the SCO summit held in Tashkent on 17 June 2004 which discussed problems related to deepening of multi-faceted cooperation within the framework of the organization. The Executive Committee of the RATS was also formally inaugurated. This marked the completion of the formation of the executive organs of the SCO although in a de facto manner. The Secretariat of the RATS and the Executive committee had already started functioning since 15 January 2004 when an extraordinary meeting of the Council of Foreign Ministers of the SCO member states was held.[4]

With the creation of the legal and normative base and operationalization of its working mechanism, the SCO began to function as a full-fledged international organization. The vertical organizational structure was fully formalized with provisions for regular meetings of the Council of Heads of States, Heads of Governments and Council of Foreign Ministers besides councils of other organizational bodies. The Charter of the SCO has been registered with the secretariat of the UN and the SCO has the status of an observer in the UN General Assembly.

SCO's Advance Towards a Credible Regional Organization

Shorn of rhetorics the SCO, despite its numerous meetings of heads of state and government, foreign ministers and defence ministers, not to speak of experts and working groups and heads of law enforcement agencies, remained in its infancy at least until 2006. Faced with various teething problems, as a Russian scholar observed, It is "yet to go a long way to find its niche in the system of international organization to demonstrate that it has its own sphere of activity where its members do not threaten any one but at the same time resolve tasks which could not have been resolved without the creation of the organization and outside its framework."[5]

As mentioned above the aims and objectives of the SCO as laid down in its Charter are quite comprehensive and ambitious. It has to demonstrate its capability to make its significant contribution to the efforts of the international community to ensure security and accelerate economic development of the region and also development of its culture.

After the founding summit in St. Petersburg followed by 2003 Moscow summit which made a notable contribution towards putting in place its organizational structure, it is only with the Tashkent summit held in 2004 that the SCO made a real start in terms of taking some important initiatives towards realization of its grandiose task. The Tashkent summit of heads of states has manifested the organization's drive to act as an instrument for Asian integration. The heads of states expressed satisfaction on the timely launch of the SCO permanent bodies—the Secretariat in Beijing and the Executive Committee of the Regional Anti-Terrorist structures (RATS) in Tashkent and noted the significant efforts of China and Uzbekistan for creating appropriate conditions for their energetic functioning. The Tashkent summit also noted that the RATS had developed concrete working plans and prepared a number of legal documents thus creating the necessary pre-conditions for its effective functioning.

The Tashkent summit of the SCO noted the importance of the working of mechanism for financing SCO activities. It also highlighted the importance of a long-term programme of multilateral trade and economic cooperation of the SCO member states approved by the Council of Heads of States and Governments in Beijing in September 2003. This document contains a common understanding of business partnership, goals and tasks of the six countries up to 2020. It also outlines ways and means for their mobilization. The Tashkent summit also lauded the protocol on cooperation and coordination of activity among ministers of foreign affairs of the six countries. It expressed the hope that the Council of Foreign Ministers would play an important role in coordinating the position of member states on urgent issues of international life. It also supported the initiative of Uzbekistan on holding regular meetings of Security Council secretariat of the member states of the organization. The Tashkent summit while emphasizing the importance of the work of the Council of National Coordinators of the SCO also surged this body to engage itself in the task of elaboration of conceptual approaches to the further development of the SCO.

The heads of SCO member states in their Tashkent meeting endorsed the principle of openness followed by the SCO and adopted the regulations of the observer status of the SCO aimed at expanding SCO contacts with other international associations and states, regardless of their geographical positions. The cooperation of the SCO with all regional associations in the Asia-Pacific region came in for a particular mention in the Tashkent declaration of the heads of states of the SCO. It recommended gradual creation of a partnership network of multilateral associations by concluding among them corresponding agreements including granting each other on mutual basis the observer status. The Tashkent summit expressed the hope that realization of this initiative would promote the formation of a co-operation system of regional security within the framework of the UN Charter and international law based on equal consideration of interests of participants of all the states.

The declaration adopted at the Tashkent summit of the SCO made an important contribution to improve the global security scenario by proclaiming that "the SCO is ready to actively participate in constructive formation of a new architecture of security capable of consolidating wide international efforts for counteracting new challenges and threats to global and regional stability". The Summit further stated, "To achieve these goals the SCO will cooperate with other states and international structures, first of all with the UNO, to contribute to security and stability not only in the SCO region but the world in general.

The Tashkent summit of the SCO also came out with constructive suggestions for forming a global system of fight against terrorism under the aegis of the United Nations. It also highlighted the need for work on prevention of terrorist activities. The summit recommended joint anti-terrorist exercises with the participation of law enforcement agencies and special services.

The SCO meet in Tashkent in its Declaration characterized the "progressive economic development of the Central Asian region and contiguous states as well as satisfaction of essential vital needs of the population as guarantees of their security and stability. The heads of states also emphasized the time bound implementation of measures for trade and economic cooperation through increase in goods turnover, harmonization of normative legal base, gradually creating favourable conditions for free movement of goods and capital and technological services. It enjoined upon the four experts groups to come out with specific recommendations for progress in this direction. It also recommended the creation of the SCO

Development Fund and setting up of the SCO Business Council within shortest possible time.[6]

The Summit of Heads of States held in Astana in July 2005 represents an important milestone in the progress of the organization towards its further consolidation and maturity. It underscored the importance of the meetings of the secretaries of the National Security Council members (the second meeting was held in Astana during June 2005). The declaration issued after the Astana summit recommended to set-up an institution of permanent representatives of the member states for fulfillment of the Shanghai RATS Executive Council based in Tashkent.

The new body was to be based on the same principles on which the permanent representatives' bodies of the SCO are functioning. It expressed the hope that the next Moscow meeting of Heads of government due for autumn 2005 will provide the momentum for realization of the Action Plan on the fulfillment of the Programme of multilateral trade and economic cooperation between the SCO member states, for getting down to a more practical interaction between ministries and departments responsible for trade and economic activities. The summit also called upon the member states to establish a common SCO development fund. The Astana meeting also noted that the grant of observer status in the SCO—TO Iran, India and Pakistan would expand the organization's opportunity in terms of developing multilateral and mutually beneficial relations in various directions.[7]

The Astana declaration of December 2004 welcomed the obtaining by the SCO of observer status at the UN General Assembly and the subsequent signing of the memorandum of understanding between the SCO and CIS states and the SCO and ASEAN states. In view of the contradictory process of globalization the SCO Declaration gave a cal for "multilateral cooperation based on the principles of equal rights and mutual respect for non-interference in internal affairs." It also called upon the members of international community, irrespective of their differences of ideology and social structure to form a new concept of security based on mutual trust, mutual benefit, and mutual-non interference in internal affairs, equality and mutual benefit.

The Astana summit had at the centre of its attention the problem of refining the tools of fighting against terrorism, extremism and separatism. It recommended a close cooperation between diplomatic, foreign, external economic and law enforcement bodies, intelligence and defence bodies of the member states as well as joint planning and conduct of anti-terrorist activities. It also drew attention to formation of an effective mechanism of mass media, and cooperative action against new challenges and threats. The need for formulation of united approaches to counteract financing of terrorism and extremism was also highlighted by the summit which declared cooperation on tackling illicit circulation of narcotics, a matter of high priority. The SCO heads declared their readiness to participate in the international efforts on the formation of an anti-narcotic belt around Afghanistan.

The Astana declaration outlined a new approach towards outside military presence on the territory of member states of its organization. Without specifically naming America or other western powers, it called upon respective member states of the anti-terrorist coalition to set up a time frame for their temporary use of military bases and status of their military contingents.

Recommending interaction within the SCO framework in areas such as education, culture, sports and tourism, the SCO heads of states also emphasized formulation of coordinated action on the part of member states. The SCO heads of states again reiterated that "expanding the organization's potential does not hurt the interest of other states and does not mean a movement towards creation of a bloc".

As already discussed the situation in Afghanistan after the Taliban takeover which converted the country into a nursery for the cultivation of terrorism under the banner of militant Islam, acted as a catalytic agent for the emergence of the SCO. However, the induction of the American military bases and military personnel on the territory of the Central Asian states to facilitate fight against international terrorism under the aegis of international coalition against international terrorism in Afghanistan also resulted in the cooling off of the ardour for regional cooperation among a section of political elites of Central Asia. This had a destabilizing effect on the development of the SCO in its initial period. The political elites of Central Asia welcomed the prospects of opening of the American umbrella before them as an alternative to providing security in the region without the participation of Russia and China. In Kyrgyzstan and Uzbekistan an opinion began to form that the initiative in the struggle against terrorism has passed over to Washington.

The recent disillusionment of the Central Asian elite which has come to suspect the real American motives has created new opportunities for development of the SCO. The creation of the SCO peacekeeping force will perhaps under the existing circumstances be more acceptable to the Central Asian leaders. In this context the demand of the SCO heads at their Astana summit in July 2005 is an ominous pointer in this direction. The Tashkent based RATS organization which is an important organ of the SCO is of late making a significant advance. The RATS has already formed a data bank on international terrorists, separatists and extremist organizations, their structures, leaders and participants.

It has also collected information on the financial sources of these forces and drafted various international legal documents relating to the struggle against terrorism. In the second session of the Council of RATS a plan for organizing cooperation for anti-terrorist struggle under the auspices of SCO for the period 2004-2006 was confirmed. Member states of the SCO have forged cooperation among their defence forces to cope with the threat of terrorism. In August 2003 in the border region of Kazakhstan and China an anti-terrorist exercise was conducted in which more than 1,000 servicemen of member states participated.

Although a major breakthrough in the development of the SCO is yet to be achieved and the SCO Development Fund and Business Council are still in the pipeline, it cannot be denied that the concerned ministries and departments have been actively engaged in this endeavour beginning with the first meeting of the heads of governments which was held at Almaty in September 2001. This meeting resulted in the signing of a memorandum by the members of SCO on the basic aims and directions of regional economic cooperation. Ministers of trade and foreign economic relations met in May 2002 in Shanghai and again in 2003 in Bishkek. In September 2003 in the meeting of Council of Heads of Governments of SCO member states held in Beijing adopted a Programme of multifaceted trade and economic cooperation among the SCO members. The document lays down the basic indicators and stage of economic integration under the framework of SCO for the period up to 2020. Meetings of experts took place in Moscow and Tashkent during 2004 to make recommendations for implementing this programme. In October 2002 the SCO Forum on Investment in the sphere of Energy met in Beijing.

In Bishkek at the Council of Heads of Governments meeting in September 2004 more than hundred concrete projects were earmarked for completion through cooperation among member states of the SCO. Plans were prepared in the sphere of creation of an international transport corridor.

In the cultural sphere also some important steps have been undertaken. The Bishkek meeting of Council of Heads of governments highlighted the need for activisation of cooperation within the framework of SCO in the sphere of education, culture, public health and tourism which would further strengthen ties of friendship among member states.

Notwithstanding multitude of problems, this organization is steadily albeit slowly converting itself into a prestigious functional body for resolving disputes in the region. As President Putin said, "The process of developing mechanisms for working together and resolving practical tasks has taken the Shanghai Cooperation Organisation to a completely new level of cooperation. I would draw your attention to the objectives set out at the organization's summit in Astana and also to the fact that economic cooperation is becoming an increasingly important part of our organization's work. At the same time, we remain committed to our focus on the very important part of our cooperation that is ensuring the security of our citizens. In this respect I must say a few words about the Shanghai Cooperation Organisation's efforts aimed at combating terrorism. The organization has set up special structures to work on these most complex and important tasks facing practically all civilized nations today. We have established a regional anti-terrorist organization based in Tashkent. A number of events, including in the Shanghai Cooperation Organisation member states—I am referring to the events in Uzbekistan and the recent events in Nalchik in the Russian

Federation—show that these tasks and this issue are very relevant indeed and call for our attention."[8]

The Shanghai Summit of the Heads of States of Shanghai Cooperation Organisation which marked the fifth anniversary of the founding of the Organisation may be viewed as an important milestone in the transformation of the Organisation into an effective and credible instrument of regional cooperation. If before this summit the organization had been largely preoccupied with the setting-up of its various organs and agencies and drawing up the necessary legal documents for their functioning, it is from the fifth summit held in Shanghai in 2006 that a new activation in the direction of achieving a multi-faceted regional cooperation based on a concrete plan of action can be seen.

The summit infused a new dynamism in the Secretariat of the SCO. The designation of the Head of the Secretariat was changed to Secretary General of the organisation. Bulat K. Nurgaliev from Kazakhstan was designated as the Secretary General of the Organisation for the period 2007-2009. The Heads of States met with the participants of the Inaugural Meeting of the SCO Business Council and attended the opening ceremony of the Art Festival of the SCO Member States.

The statement of the Heads of the Member States of the SCO on International Information Security was approved at the Shanghai Summit along with the new version of the SCO Secretariat and a cooperation plan of SCO members on combating terrorism, separatism and extremism for the period 2007-2009. The Shanghai Summit declared that the top priority of the Organization was to combat the threats posed by terrorism, separatism and extremism as well as illegal drug trafficking which, have not diminished but aggravated in scale and degree".

The Heads of SCO member countries commended the joint anti-terrorism military exercises within the territory of the SCO member states and expressed confidence that these would help enhance the efficiency of the member states' joint anti-terrorism operations. The summit also spoke positively of the work done by the SCO Regional Anti-Terrorist Structure (RATS).[9]

The Heads of States of the SCO at their meeting in Shanghai also pointed out that there was already a legal basis and an organizational structure for carrying out economic cooperation. They declared that establishment of the SCO Business Council and the Inter Bank Association would greatly enhance the development of economic cooperation under the organization which would also be facilitated by the credit fund of $900 million provided by China. All member states agreed to give priority to cooperation in the field of energy, information technology and transportation which had entered the stage of pilot projects.

The Shanghai SCO summit emphasized the importance of promoting the work of SCO with the help of non-governmental organizations and hailed the SCO interparliamentary initiative. It also welcomed the initiative endorsed by the SCO summit at Tashkent in 2004 on establishing cooperative relations among international organization in the Asia Pacific region and noted with satisfaction that documents for cooperation between the SCO and ASEAN, the CISI and Eurasian Economic Community (EURASEC).

The seventh SCO summit held in Bishkek in August 2007 discussed in an in-depth manner the current regional and international issues. Carrying forward the line of the previous summits for expanding the organization's activities in cooperation with the legislative and judicial bodies of the member states, the Bishkek summit recommended active exchange of information in the field of legislation and dispensation of justice. The leaders drew attention to the urgency of fight against terrorism and emphasize the need for taking of precautionary measures to tackle threats against peace, security and stability. They agreed to step up efforts to crack down on illegal immigration, drug trafficking and terrorism. The possibilities of the SCO playing a larger role in Afghanistan affairs to contribute to regional security and stability were discussed at the summit.

The Bishkek summit reiterated the energy cooperation among the SCO members and hoped they would hold the common ground on the issues. The international exchanges of the SCO with other countries and organizations came in for appreciation at the summit which also noted the importance of strengthening concrete cooperation with SCO observers in various fields.[10] The Bishkek summit attracted attention on account of participation of the Turkmen President Gurbangully Berdymukhamedov as guest of the host country.[11] The Bishkek summit also lent support to the urgency of the UN reforms, first and foremost relating to the Security Council. It emphasized that the reforms should be carried out on the basis of wider consensus of its members. The SCO Member states at their Bishkek meet called for non-proliferation of weapons of mass destruction. It came out in support of urgent steps to draft an international legal document on preventing the deployment of weapons in outer space, use of force or the threat of using force against space objects.[12]

The Bishkek SCO meet of Heads of states noted the significance of the Central Asia Nuclear-Weapon-Free Zone Treaty (Semiplatinsk, 8 September 2006) and welcomed the adoption at the 61st session of the UN General Assembly of a resolution highly evaluating the contribution of the Central Asian States to the cause of nuclear non-proliferation regime.

At Bishkek, on 16 August 2007, an important treaty on Long-Term Good-Neighbourliness, Friendship and Cooperation between Member states of the Shanghai Cooperation Organisation was signed. This treaty shall be subject to registration with the UN Secretariat in accordance with article 102 of the UN Charter. The treaty reaffirmed the readiness of the parties to expand mutually beneficial cooperation among them and with all interested states and international organizations to promote a just and rational world order, creating favourable conditions for a sustainable development of the Organization's Member States. The treaty states that it was not directed against any states or organizations and that the contracting parties shall follow the principle of openness to the other countries of the world. The parties pledged themselves to work for making the SCO space a region of peace, Cooperation, prosperity and harmony. They declared their intention to contribute to more democratic international relations and to the establishment of a new architecture of a global security on the basis of equality, mutual respect, mutual trust and benefit, as well as abrogation of a bloc based and ideological division.[13] The signatories to the treaty stated that they were to be guided by the goals and principles of the UN Charter, universally recognized principles and norms of international law as well as by the Charter of the Shanghai Cooperation organization of 7 June 2002.[14]

If the focus of the Bishkek SCO Summit was on fight against terrorism and increase cooperation among the legislative and judicial bodies of the member states, the summit held in Dushanbe, the Capital of Tajikistan, had at the Centre of its discussion the issue of security and energy. This was the first summit to be attended by the new Russian President Dmitry Medvedev.

The Dushanbe summit totally rejected the use of force as a means of resolving international conflicts. Recommending a comprehensive approach to security the seventh SCO summit favoured "taking into account the interests of all parties involved and including them all in the negotiation process rather than isolating any of them."[15] The Dushanbe declaration on security, energy and other issues decried the approach of strengthening a country's own security at the expanse of that of others. It described such an approach as detrimental to maintaining global security and stability.[16] The SCO members at their Dushanbe summit reiterated their efforts to maintain the Central coordinating role of the United Nations in the global fight against terrorism and to steadfastly implement the UN Global Counter-Terrorism Strategy. It also called for finalization of a Comprehensive convention on fighting global terrorism at an early date.[17]

The Dushanbe summit also discussed the creation of a global anti-missile defence system and noted that establishment of such a system would not help in maintaining a strategic balance and that it was inconsistent with international efforts towards arms control and nuclear non-proliferation. It further stated that such an approach was not conducive to enhancing trust among countries and regional stability. On the question of South Ossetia the SCO members expressed their deep concern over the tension triggered by this conflict and called on concerned parties to solve it through dialogue.[18]

The summit also urged SCO members to forge close cooperation in developing new energy technology against the backdrop of global climate change. It also suggested that the

SCO members develop environment-friendly clean energy. The on-going global economic crisis was also discussed at this summit. It urged measures to ensure that all countries equally enjoy the benefit of globalization. To achieve this end it was necessary in its view to implement responsible fiscal and financial policies, monitor capital flows and ensure food and energy security. The summit also recommended that the SCO members conduct dialogue on the efficient use of water resources.[19]

The Georgian invasion of South Ossetia was discussed at the Dushanbe summit. Although the official SCO position as stated in the Dushanbe Declaration on Security, Energy and other issues was a call to the parties to resolve problems peacefully through dialogue, press reports about behind the door discussions indicated general support for the Russian stand. It was reported that in his one-to-one meeting with Russian President Medvedev, Kazakhstan President Nazarbayev told him that his country "understands and supports the measures taken by Russia".[20] Nazarbayev also informed his Russian counterpart that he was "amazed at the West's failure to acknowledge the fact that it was Georgian armed forces who attacked peaceful civilian in Tskhinvali". Nazarbayev further added that "this started the conflict, and Russia's all subsequent actions were aimed at stopping the blood shed".[21] While the SCO leaders refrained from condemning Georgia's attack on the breakaway territory of South Ossetia, their solidarity with Russia stood in stark contrast with the West denunciation of the "Russian aggression" against Georgia and the call of EU summit to punish Russia.[22] The Dushanbe meet of the SCO states in the joint declaration issued by it welcomed the adoption in Moscow on August 12 of six principles of settling the conflict in South Ossetia. It also supported Russia's "active role in contributing to peace and cooperation in the region'.[23]

The discussions at the Dushanbe summit were of great importance for promotion of economic cooperation in the region, raising the status of the Observer states, creation of the Energy Club and strengthening the Afghanistan Contact Group. A memorandum on partnership between the SCO Interbank Association and the Eurasian Development Bank was signed. The work with the SCO observer states, India, Iran, Pakistan and Mongolia was put on a qualitatively new level. The SCO Heads of States approved the Regulations on the Status of Dialogue Partner of the SCO: Through the years, geopolitics and lingering mutual fears by China, Russia and the four Central Asian States have kept the group from expanding further. The induction of Dialogue Partner may be seen as an important step in changing this. The President of Kazakhstan, Nazarbayev expressed his strong support for the SCO Energy Club. Nazarbayev was reported to have stated at the summit: "it is absolutely necessary to draw up a common energy strategy as soon as possible. There are all components for setting an energy community in the SCO, within whose framework the interests of producers, shippers, and consumers of energy resources can be harmonized".[24]

Following the recommendation of the Dushanbe Meet of SCO states to strengthen the Afghanistan Contact Group, a conference was held in Moscow in March 2009 under the aegis of the organization to discuss matters relating to fight against terrorism, illicit drug trafficking and organized crime. Beside the six member states of SCO, the Islamic Republic of Afghanistan also participated in the conference. The SCO conference on Afghanistan welcomed the efforts of the Afghan

Government to decrease cultivation of opium. It also expressed concern about the continued cultivation and production of narcotic drugs as a source of financing terrorist activities in Afghanistan, the region and abroad.

The Conference called upon all states concerned to implement, in the framework of the United Nations activities, and other international and regional organizations, existing international strategies to combat narcotics in Afghanistan. Calling for strict implementation of resolution 1817 of UN Security Council, it also suggested creating and reinforcing of the "anti-drug and financial security belts"[25] in the region.

The SCO conference on Afghanistan suggested improvement of international legal framework, in particular, early elaboration and adoption of a comprehensive convention on international terrorism as well as the elaboration of regional counter-terrorism legal instruments. The conference gave a call for adherence to relevant resolutions of the UN Security Council. It stated: "We call for stopping the attempts to spread terrorist ideology as well as for strict compliance with the UN Security Council Resolution 1624 (2005), which condemns all acts of terrorism irrespective of their motivation, and call upon member states to prohibit by law terrorist acts and incitement to commit such acts, as well as to deny safe haven to those guilty of committing these acts". The conference suggested international, inter-ethnic and inter-religious dialogue in order to fight terrorist ideology. It called for the involvement of the civil society including religious leaders, mass media, business communities and educational structures. The conference reiterated the intention of the SCO Member States to invest more efforts in combating the terrorist threat, using the capacity of the SCO Regional Anti-Terrorism Structure to a greater extent and the practice of joint SCO counter-terrorism exercises. It invited observer states and other countries concerned in the collective efforts, including those related to creating the anti-terrorist security belt, and consider taking part in transiting non-military cargoes needed by International Security Assistance force in Afghanistan (ISAF).[26]

Following the highly successful Dushanbe SCO summit which galvanized the organization to step up its activities in the field of ensuring security and energy related cooperation besides a heightened interest in the fight against terrorism and drug trafficking in Afghanistan, the next SCO summit was held in the Russian city of Yekaterinburg in June 2009. In many ways this latest summit is an important land mark in the history of the SCO. The Yekaterinburg summit deliberated on issues of great relevance in the prevailing international environment. The very fact that the convening of this SCO summit in Russia almost simultaneously attracted a number of other international events—the BRIC summit and visit of US President Obama to Russia in the region was indicative of the rising significance of the Eurasian region in the context of the current world economic crisis climate change and the intensified global struggle against terrorism.

In terms of the level of participation, the Yekaterinburg summit set a new record. The President of the Republic of Kazakhstan, N. Nazarbayev, Chairman of the peoples' Republic of China, Hu Jintao, President of the Republic of Kyrgyzstan, K. Bakiev, President of the Russian Federation D. Medvedev, President of the Republic of Tajikistan E. Rakhmon and President of the Republic of Uzbekistan I. Karimov took part in the summit chaired by the Russian President. Heads of delegations from the Observer states included the Prime Minister of India, Manmohan Singh, President of the Islamic Republic of Iran, M. Ahmadinejad, President of the Islamic

Republic of Pakistan A. Zardari and first Vice-Premier of Mongolia N. Altankhuyag. President of the Islamic Republic of Afghanistan H. Karzai, UN Under Secretary General N. Pascoe were also present as guest of the host state besides Chairman of the Executive Committee of the CIS S. Lebedev, Secretary General of the Eurasian Economic Committee. T. Mansurov, Secretary General of the CSTO N. Bordyuzha. The Secretary of the SCO B. Nurgaliev and Director of the Executive Committee of the SCO Regional Anti-terrorism Structure M. Subanov were also present.

Active participation at the highest level of the Observer states was an unprecedented new feature of this summit. Over the years the SCO Observer countries, India, Iran, Pakistan and Mongolia have shown their interest to join the Organisation as full members. As far back as 2002 when the basic documents of the Organisation were adopted at St. Petersburg, President Putin had revealed that India was exploring the possibilities of participating in a wide range of SCO activities through Foreign Ministers' Channel. Yashwant Sinha, the then Foreign Minister of India was reported to have said, "India believes that the SCO fulfils important tasks, especially in the struggle against the threat of terrorism. India is interested in joining the SCO and had notified Russia and other member states of her intention. Our membership in the SCO does not depend on whether any other country is or is not going to join this structure. We believe that India could contribute considerably to the SCO activities. However, we realize as well that at the present moment its admission regulations make it difficult to become new member. Nevertheless we watch its activities attentively".[27] Subsequently, Indian External Affairs Minister K. Natwar Singh announced a month after the Astana summit, "To deepen engagement with the region, India plans to apply for the full membership of the SCO."[28]

In fact, the problem of expansion of the SCO by admission of new members had been engaging the attention of previous summits. The consensus was that as there was no unanimity of opinion among the member states on this question, it may better be deferred till such time as a general consensus was achieved. It was reported in the media that China did not favour membership of India while Russia and Kazakhstan were favourably inclined. In fact the presidents of Russia and Kazakhstan had publicly endorsed the SCO membership of India. There seemed to be differences among the SCO members on the entry of Iran in View of hostile US reaction. It may be recalled that the Dushanbe Summit had come up with a solution of this problem by mooting out a new concept of dialogue partners for upgrading the observer status. It had openly invited observer countries of the SCO to take part in the anti-terrorist military exercises by the RATS. The SCO Moscow conference on Afghanistan had also invited the observer countries to participate as equals along with the SCO members in the Organisation's initiative to create a security and financial belt around Afghanistan to bring peace and stability in that country.

As noted above the current global economic and financial situation received serious attention at the Yekaterinburg summit. The Declaration adopted at the summit stressed "the need to increase cooperation of the international community in the field of controlling and managing international finances, making joint efforts to prevent the growth and spread of financial crisis risks, maintaining economic stability. It announced that "the member states of the Organisation together with the international community intend to make efforts for the formation of more just, equal, all-embracing and well-regulated international financial regime which takes into account a true balance of interest of all its participants and gives all states equal access to the advantages of globalization."[29] Summit recommended strengthening of sharing of information and interaction as regards the international financial sector and the issues of tackling the consequences of the global financial crisis in the SCO region. It further urged the SCO member states to bolster trade, economic and investment cooperation in the framework of the organization, including involving the potential of the Observer States and dialogue partners. (It may be mentioned that the summit accepted Sri Lanka and Belarus as dialogue partners).

The SCO summit at Yekaterinburg called for implementation of projects on international transport corridors, modernization of railways and roads which in its opinion would create preconditions for strengthening the potential of the region as a transcontinental bridge, giving a anew impulse to the development of economic links between Europe and Asia. Noting the key significance of the energy sector for successful, economic development and creation of favourable preconditions for improving the living standards of their citizens the summit reiterated the determination of the member states to further advance cooperation in this field on the basis of equality with the aim of ensuring effective, reliable and environmentally safe energy supply. The summit also called for innovative and energy saving technologies including renewable sources of energy.[30]

The SCO meet at Yekaterinburg noted the outcome of special conference on Afghanistan under SCO auspices held in Moscow in March 2009. It approved the results of seventh meeting of Defence Ministers in Moscow in April 2009, first meeting of

Ministers of internal affairs and public security held in Yekaterinburg in May 2009 and the fourth meeting of the Secretaries of Security Council in Moscow in May 2009. It decided to raise the level of coordination of cooperation of the SCO member states in fighting against terrorism and other threats in the field of security. The RATS was recommended for a central role in this field. Proceeding from the outcome of the joint counter terrorism exercise of the SCO named Norak Anti-Terror 2009 held in Tajikistan in April 2009, the parties acknowledged the expediency of continuing the practice of regular joint counter terrorism drill.[31]

Perhaps the most notable achievement of the Yekaterinburg summit was adoption by the Heads of States of the SCO Counter Terrorism Convention. In a way this anti-terrorism Convention marked the consummation of the process started by the organization right since its inception in 2001. The first SCO Shanghai summit, it may be recalled, had adopted a very important convention on combating terrorism, separatism and extremism which embodied a very elaborate and broad definition of terrorism. The convention on counter terrorism signed at Yekaterinburg cemented the legal base for counter-terrorism interaction in the SCO framework, taking the potential for cooperation in this field to a new level.[32] If the SCO became the first international organization to address seriously the problem of international terrorism nearly three months before the terrorist strike in America on 9/11, the adoption by the organization of another counter-terrorism convention in less than a decade time of its existence at a time when the international community is engaged in the final round of military campaign against terrorism in Afghanistan, speaks volumes about its contribution to the global efforts against this deadly threat to humanity and civilization.

The SCO 2009 summit also discussed the question of reform of the UN Security Council. It called for strengthening coordination among SCO member states on this question. The summit also stressed the significance of ensuring international information security as one of the key elements of the common system of international security. The summit reaffirmed its commitment to a dialogue of civilization. It also rejected the approach of gaining unilateral advantages in the field of defence as counter productive. Opposing proliferation of nuclear weapons, it stated that the basic element of international regime was the treaty of non-proliferation of nuclear weapons. It exhorted the SCO member states to work for raising the effectiveness of the treaty on the basis of the unity of its three components: non-proliferation, disarmament, peaceful use of nuclear energy. The summit also welcomed the start of the Russo-American negotiations on drafting a treaty on the Reduction of Offensive Strategic Arms. It also hailed the coming into effect on 21 March 2009 of the Treaty on Establishing a Nuclear Free Zone in Central Asia. The Declaration adopted at the summit announced that the "Organisation has become an essential element of the fledgling system of security and cooperation in the Asia Pacific region".[33]

Summing up, from the detailed narration given above of the issues taken up for consideration and important principles and policies outlined at the SCO summits from Shanghai (2001) to Yekaterinburg (2009) it is clear that the organization has come of age. It has established its niche in the history of the development of international organizations for regional security and cooperation. True, the success achieved may not be commensurate with the hopes and aspirations of the advocates of a new type of regional cooperation. The pace of progress was no doubt rather tardy, but consolation is that it was steady. In fact, for a new type of a regional security structure that the SCO is, and, considering that its membership comprises widely disparate elements with a heavy historical baggage of discord and disharmony the success achieved may be termed remarkable. Nine years is not a very long period in history to judge an organization of nations. Yet the Shanghai Cooperation Organization has numerous achievements to its credit which have been highlighted in the discussion of its summits of Heads of States and Governments, Regional Anti-Terrorist Structure, Council of Foreign Ministers and other Organs of the member States. The institutional structures for a proper and efficient functioning of an organization are already at place. The organization can justifiably claim successes in the field of fighting terrorism. The spillover of religious extremism and terrorism from Afghanistan into the contiguous areas has been effectively contained in general barring the recent acts of unrest in the Xinjiang region of China.

Construction on projects relating of roads and railways lines and progress of work on the transport corridors, albeit slow, has opened up a new perspective for the region to regain some of its old glory as the Silk Route. The organization has also been instrumental in securing and settling the borders and demilitarizing the region, thus creating an environment for peace, security and cooperation. Some progress can also be noted in the field of construction of oil pipelines. But it is still a long way to the establishment of an SCO Energy club and regional energy market. The desired goal of increased shipment of Eurasian oil and gas to the countries of the Asia-Pacific region is still a distant one and a balance between the supplies to West Europe and Asia remains a dream unrealized.

NOTES

1. Chou Gan, "Sotrudnichestvo v oblasti borby terrorizmom mezhdu Kitaem, Indiei I Rossiei", *Vzaimodeistvie Rossii, Indii i Kitaya v XXI Veke* T. 2, Moscow, IDV Ran, 2004, p. 156.
2. Charter of the SCO http://president.Kremlin.ru/text/docs/2002/06/46246.shtml.
3. *Ibid.*
4. Alexander Lukin, *Analyticheskki Zapiskii*, vyp. 2(4), February 2005, p. 12.
5. *Ibid.*
6. http://www./sectsco.org/news-details.asp?id=119 & language ID=2
7. http://www./sectsco.org/home.asp?id=119 & language ID=2; www.un.int/kazakhstan/pages_05/docs_05/doc07_13_05.htm - 27k
8. http://www.In.mid.rju/brp_4.nsf/0/e36562bf44d20f04c32570a7003e3aa7?opendocument
9. Joint Communiqué of the Meeting of the Council of Heads of Member States of Shanghai Cooperation Organisation, Shanghai, 2006; http://www.sectsco.org/En/show.asp?id95
10. Bishkek Declaration of the Heads of Member States of the Shanghai Cooperation Organisation, 16/8/2007; http://www.sectssco.org/EN/Show.asp?id=92
11. SCO summit meeting issues Joint Communiqué; http://news.Xinhuanet.com/English/2007-2008/17/content6547304.htm
12. Bishkek Declaration of the Heads of the Member states of the Shanghai Cooperation Organisation, 16/8/2007; http://www.sectsco.org/EN/show/asp?id-92.
13. Treaty on Long-Term Good-Neighbourliness, Friendship and Cooperation Between Member States of the Shanghai Cooperation Organisation, http://www.sectsco.org/En/show.asp?id=71
14. *Ibid.*
15. Dushanbe Declaration of the Heads of the Member States of the Shanghai Cooperation Organisation; http://www.sectsco.org/En/show.asp?id=90; see also, SCO leaders issue declaration on security, energy, August 29, 2008 – Peoples Daily Online http://www.English.peopledaily.com.cn/90001/90776/90883/649033/html.
16. *Ibid.*
17. *Ibid.*
18. *Ibid.*
19. *Ibid.*
20. http://www.hinduonet.com/thehindu/thscrip/print.Pl?/file=20080829

21. *Ibid.*
22. *Ibid.*
23. *Ibid.*
24. *Ibid.*
25. Statement by the Shanghai Cooperation Organisation Member States and the Islamic Republic of Afghanistan on combating terrorism, illicit drug trafficking and organized crimes 27.3.2009; http://www.sectsco.org/EN/Show.asp?id=100
26. *Ibid.*
27. Cited in Mahavir Singh, ed., Building a new Asia, 2005, Shipra, p. 9.
28. Cited in The Shanghai Cooperation Organisation: Prospects for a multipolar world by Rick Rozobb, *Global Research*, May 22, 2009.
29. Yekaterinburg Declaration of the Heads o the Member States of the Shanghai Cooperation Organisation; http://www.seatsco.org/EN/Show.asp?id=87
30. Yekaterinburg Declaration ....http://www.sectsco.org/EN/show.asp?id=87.
31. Joint Communiqué of Meeting of the Council of the Heads of the Member States of the Shanghai Cooperation Organisation; http://www.sectsco.org/EN/show.asp?id=88.
32. *Ibid.*
33. Yekaterinburg Declaration ... *op. cit.*

Four

The Shanghai Cooperation Organisation: Retrospect and Prospect

On 15 June 2009 the SCO has completed eight years of its existence. Together with its predecessor, the Shanghai-Five, it has completed more than a decade of its formation. Eight years or even a decade plus is not a long time on the scales of history. Yet, during this short period the organization has played an important part in preserving security and stability and facilitating regional cooperation in the Eurasian region.

As President Putin said in his written interview to the Chinese News Agency Xinhua, "From the perspective of history, not a lot of time has passed since the SCO was established. I would like to note that its members have not only reached the objectives they set at the time the organization was created, but have gone far beyond the initially defined goals. Today we can say that the SCO has become a full-fledged regional organization and is now expanding its work in the economy, in social and humanitarian affairs and in other areas.

"The organization is making active use of its potential for strengthening regional stability and security and for combating terrorism, separatism and extremism. What is more, we are expanding our cooperation to other countries in the region. Along with the six founding members, politically and economically important countries such as India, India, Mongolia and Pakistan have been granted observer status and have expressed their desire to take part in any joint plans. Today the organization seeks to develop forms of cooperation that would have the most positive and tangible impact on the everyday lives of the three billion people in countries which have united under its aegis."[1]

The SCO was born on 15 June 2001 as a permanent inter-governmental international organization consisting of six countries—China, Russia, Kazakhstan, Kyrgyzstan, Tajikistan and Uzbekistan. It was established on the basis of the "Shanghai Five" mechanism. The main objectives of this organization are: strengthening mutual trust and good neighbourliness among member states; promoting their effective cooperation in political affairs, economy and trade, scientific-technical, cultural and educational spheres as well as in energy, transportation, tourism and environment protection fields; joint-safeguarding and preserving of regional peace, security and stability, striving towards creation of democratic, just reasonable new international political and economic order. In the international relations, the SCO is guided by the spirit of "Shanghai Five" of mutual trust and benefit, equality, mutual consultations, respect for the multi-faceted culture and aspirations to joint development. In external relations the SCO is not a closed bloc and is not directed against any states and regions.[2] The Council of Heads of Member states is the supreme body responsible for decision making. It holds regular session once a year and makes decisions on issues relating to all the important matters of the organisation.

The Council of heads of Government of SCO member states holds a regular meeting once a year to discuss strategy of multilateral cooperation and priority directions within the SCO framework; to decide on actual matters of principle regarding economic and other cooperation, as well as to approve the next year budget of the organization. Besides, meetings of Councils of Heads of States and Heads of Governments, there also exist the mechanisms of annual meetings of Ministers of Foreign Affairs, ministers of Economy, Transport, Culture, Defense and Security, general public prosecutors as well as Heads of Border Organisation of respective member states.

The Centre of National Coordinators of SCO member states serves as the coordinating mechanism within the SCO framework. The SCO has two permanent bodies—Secretariat in Beijing and Regional Anti-Terrorist Structure (RATS) in Tashkent. The Secretary General and the Director of the Executive Committee are appointed by the Councils of Heads of States for a period of three years.[3]

What augurs well for the future of the SCO is the state of excellent bilateral relations between Russia and China. These two powerful countries registered an upward progress in their relations during 2005-06 years. Russian President Putin and Chinese President Hu Jintao met with each other four times within 2005. Recently in 2005 the tenth regular meeting of the two prime ministers was held in Beijing. The high-level mutual visits of the two sides have enhanced the personal friendship, mutual trust and understanding between the top-leadership of the two countries. China and Russia share a 4,300 km border. During the talks in Vladivostok in June 2005 Chinese Foreign Minister Li Zhaoxing and his Russian counterpart Sergei

Lavrov exchanged ratification documents over the eastern border thus putting an end to 40 years of negotiations.

In China the year of Russia was celebrated during 2006, followed by China year in Russia in 2007. The two cultural programmes covered a wide spectrum of areas including culture, education, economy, political system and traditional customs.[4] The China year in Russia which was celebrated with great zeal and gusto in 2007 included large number of programmes such as cultural festivals and exhibitions and a ceremony marking the anniversary of the establishment of the diplomatic ties. More and more Russian people are getting increasingly interested in the Chinese culture and are eager to learn Chinese language. The daughters of President Putin as he himself recalled in his address in the Russian-Chinese Business Communities, Economic Forum in Beijing on 22 March 2006 are studying Chinese martial arts and one of them as Putin disclosed in his interview to Xinhua agency, is studying Chinese language. Knowing Chinese language, as president Putin stated, "has become the key to success for many Russian business men, opening up to them not just the market in your country but also enabling them to work effectively in many countries in the Asia-Pacific region where members of the Chinese overseas community have established strong economic position."[5]

Bilateral trade between Russia and China exceeded $20 billion mark in 2004 rising to $29 billion in 2005. Russia's trade with China has been growing considerably faster than the Russian Federation's trade in general. Russia was in that year one of the top trading partners of China. Mutual investments have also shown a confident growth. 19 Chinese investment projects in the Russian Federation have been cleared with a total investment of $2 billion. Russia's investment in China exceeds $500 million.

On the eve of his March 2006 visit to Beijing president Putin stated that the Russian Federation had taken a decision to build a pipeline system from Eastern Siberia to the Pacific Coast and Russian and Chinese organizations were discussing the question of building a branch pipeline to connect this system to China. Cooperation between the Russian Gazprom and the CNPC is forging ahead in the field of gas supplies to China where underground gas reservoirs are being built and options for building gas pipelines are also being explored. Various projects of cooperation for construction of a number of electricity generation plants in Russia and subsequent supplies to the Chinese market are under discussion.[6]

The leaders of the two countries pledged at least to double the level of trade by 2010. The Russia-China relationship reached a new height in July 2005 when in a meeting between President Putin and his Chinese counterpart Hu Jintao, a joint declaration on the international order in the 21st century was adopted. With the signing of thc document which President Putin termed as a "system-building document", the solid relationship between the two countries has already become an important factor in maintaining global stability. Both countries are firm supporters of building a genuinely democratic system of international relations based on equality of opportunity for all countries large and small. President Putin in his interview cited above described relations with China as based on "genuine partnership" underpinned by a solid legal foundation, above all by the Treaty of Good-Neighbourliness, Friendship and Cooperation signed in 2001.[7]

The relations between Russia and China reached a new unprecedented level in August 2005 when the two countries held a joint military exercise named "Peaceful mission-2005" under the aegis of the SCO. The conduct of a high profile military exercise showed the long path covered by the SCO which began as an anti-terrorist organisation. Most Western editorial comments on this exercise noted that its purpose was to serve notice to Washington that Moscow and Beijing could not accept US military supremacy in the Far East in the long-run. The two countries conducted a joint military exercise that involved about 10,000 soldiers, most of whom were Chinese. Besides naval ships and submarines, Russian Tu-22 backfire long range bombers and T.U.95 "Bears" Intercontinental bombers participated in the exercise.[8] Russian Daily *Nezavisimaya Gazeta* projected this exercise as "above all an assault on the uni-polar world that has so suited Washington since the end of the Cold War".

Jim Canrogh, Professor of International Relations at people's University of China also observed that the "main target is the united States". Both sides want to improve their bargaining positions in terms of security, politics and economics". *Pravda Ru* pointed out that "the reconciliation between China and Russia has been driven in part by mutual unease at US power and fear of Islamic extremism in Central Asia". Russia and China held new military exercises in 2007, this time in southern Russia. The joint exercises included Special Forces from China's Public Security Ministry. The exercises according to Russian Interior Minister were expected to "develop skills for cooperation in accomplishing objectives to counter the threat of terrorism".

The August 2005 Sino-Russian joint military exercises in the Far East under the SCO involving strategic bombers and sub marines and marine landing operations have little relevance to the anti-terrorist operations for which the organization was primarily created. They are bound to give rise to speculations about the intended conversion of the SCO into a military bloc.

With the subsequent purchase by China of the Russian made IL-76 transport planes and IL-78 refueling tankers and submarine class destroyers these speculations have been further strengthened. American military observers Ariel Cohen and John J. Tkacik Jr. have viewed the Sino-Russian war games in 2005 as a "logical outcome of the Sino-Russian Treaty of Good Neighbourly Friendship and Cooperation signed in 2001 and the shared world view and growing economic ties between the two Great Powers".[9]

To counteract it the American specialists suggested "strengthening of military, security and economic cooperation with India and Japan including cooperation in joint business projects in the Russian Far East and Central Asia. Other measures recommended by them included securing an observer status in the SCO and use of US public diplomacy to focus attention on the problems inherent in closer Sino-Russian relations.[10] Cohen and Tkacik suggested pursuit of pro-active policies aimed at preventing the bear and the dragon from getting closer.

Moscow has, however, hastened to deny that there are plans to forge a military bloc out of the SCO. Russian Defence Minister Sergei Ivanov announced in Beijing after attending the SCO Ministerial meet in May 2006 that "the SCO will not turn into a military-political alliance, at least in the near future". According to Russian Defence Minister Sergei Ivanov the SCO goal is to maintain stability and security on the territory within its jurisdiction. The Russian Defence Minister further noted that the SCO "does not conceal its military activities" which were "rather limited". Unlike the NATO, he asserted, the SCO does not have in its charter a provision on the collective defence of its members by others in the event of an outside attack. The SCO military components stipulate collective resistance to big armed gangs of multinational terrorists if they cross the borders of a member country. The military components further stipulate that "Our task is to block them on both sides and start destroying them" said Sergei Ivanov. "To be able to do it quickly, we must conduct exercises"—Ivanov emphasized. He claimed that Russo-Chinese exercises in 2005 had an anti-terrorist status. Ivanov also disclosed that Russia and Uzbekistan were to conduct similar exercises in the mountains in 2006. Similar exercises involving all the SCO member states were held in 2006 on the territory of Volga-Uralsk military districts near the town of Chebarkul.[11]

Russian military commentator Viktor Litovkin also connected the Indian air base in Aini in Tajikistan with the anti-drug and anti-terrorist operations in Afghanistan and Central Asia in collaboration with the Russian air base in Kant (Kyrgyzstan). This was attributed by him to India's interest as an observer in the SCO in the anti-terrorist activities in Central Asia and the adjacent regions which are a source of threat to its security as well. The Russian analysts in his write up also mentioned about Iran's inclination to change its observer status for full membership of the SCO against the background of the US threat of an attack to stall its nuclear programme. But Sergei Ivanov, Russian Defence Minister emphatically denied any move to admit Iran. He stated in Beijing Iran was an observer in the SCO and nobody in the SCO had any obligations to defend it. At the same time he reiterated the policy of Russia and China to work for a peaceful resolution of the problem of Iran's nuclear programme through diplomatic efforts. Russia's defence Minister Sergei Ivanov in his statement in Beijing in May 2006 set at rest the speculations about admission of new members in the SCO which followed the Secretary General Zhang Deguang's statement that the SCO summit scheduled for 15 June 2006 would consider applications for full membership from countries that currently held observer status in the organisation.[12] The Secretary General like the Russian Defence Minister also denied any plan to convert the SCO into a military bloc.

The Beijing Session of SCO's Defence Ministers' meet in May 2006 actively discussed the status of other members besides Iran. Pakistan has officially applied and India has unofficially expressed its intention to join the SCO. However the official SCO representative took an evasive stand over the possible expansion of the organization.

The SCO Secretary General Deguang stated that "many SCO members are for its intensive, but not extensive development, now is not the best time to expand the organisation as it might hinder its effectiveness".[13] It was reported that China actively supported Pakistan's intention to join the SCO while Russia was inclined to concede this only if India is accepted at the same time. According to Russian Daily *Kommersant* Beijing also hosted talks between Moscow, Dushanbe and Delhi concerning the establishment of an Indian base at Aini in Tajikistan with 12 MiG-29 planes. Belarus was also reported to be interested in the membership of the SCO but it was not favoured as Belarus was not a Eurasian country like Russia which is both European and Asian.[14]

The SCO Secretary General Zhang Deguang while addressing the Russian Duma's session to commemorate the 10th anniversary of "Shanghai Five" in April 2006, observed that five year history of SCO had shown the whole world that this new international organisation had a powerful potential and huge development prospects. An increasing number of states and international organizations have a positive perception of the organization, Zhang Deguang claimed in the same address. In 2004 the SCO was granted observer status at the UN General Assembly. This paved the way for development of its ties with the UNDP, the ESCAP, the UN Counter-Terrorisms Committee and other UN institutions. In 2005 the SCO signed a MOU with the CIS Executive Committee and the ASEAN. In the framework of the recently launched SCO-Afghanistan contact group the organization started cooperation with Afghanistan. It is actively interacting with various NGOs in the member countries and has succeeded in establishing inter-parliamentary contacts. In May 2006 the first meeting of speakers of parliaments of the SCO member states was held in Moscow.

The Shanghai Cooperation Organization which appeared on the international scene as the "Shanghai Five" mechanism with the objective of resolving the border problems between China and Russia and the three Central Asian Republics as highlighted in the previous chapters, has made a significant contribution to improvement of the security situation in Central Asia with its confidence building measures and de-militarization of the border areas in the region. It has been recently increasingly focusing on regional economic cooperation among the six member states.

The SCO countries have a large potential for mutually beneficial cooperation in trade and investment in industrial and infrastructural development which has remained unrealized so far. The SCO countries have been performing well in their economies which have been developing at 6.8 per cent growth rate. China's growth rate during the three years (2003-2006) stood at above 9 percent, Russia's GDP grew in 2005 by 6.4 percent, Kazakhstan has registered a growth of 9 percent annually during the 2003-2006 period while Tajikistan's growth was 8 percent and that of Uzbekistan 7 percent. Trade turnover of SCO in 2003 was 19.7 billion dollars. During the first five months of 2004 it had gone up by 68.7 percent over the same period during the preceding year. Nevertheless, trade volume in absolute figures was far from significant.

According to a study conducted by Yevgeny Kozhokhin (Director, Russian Institute for Strategic Studies) China was at the first place among SCO members to have steadily increased its trade with the countries included in the organization. Russia-China trade reached $29.1 billion in 2005, up by 37.1 percent over 2004. In 2005 Russian and Kazakh trade was $10 billion and Russia-Kyrgyz $543 million. According to scholars contributing to this study, China increasingly claims the role of the SCO economic leader. Beijing's role in the energy and transport projects in the neighbouring countries of Kazakhstan and Turkmenistan has been steadily growing. China is concentrating its efforts on the economic development of its Western and Central provinces. Trade and economic cooperation between the Xinjiang-Uighur Autonomous Region and neighbouring Central Asian Republics has grown substantially during recent years. In 2005 SCO Central Asian countries accounted for as much as two-third of Xinjiang's foreign trade, Kazakhstan being at the first place.[15]

In 2001 the SCO member states signed the memorandum on goals and areas of regional economic cooperation and on launching measures to ensure favourable conditions for trade and investment. In 2003 the SCO adopted a programme of trade and economic cooperation. Its long-term goal for 2020 is to form a new integrated economic space, in order to gradually ensure free movement of goods, capital, services and technologies within the SCO. It provides for creation of a SCO free trade zone in the future.

In 2004 the SCO adopted an action plan with 127 clauses, out of which 19 are related to energy cooperation, 20 to transport cooperation and about one third to education, science and technology. Energy production, development of new oil and gas fields and pipelines are a priority area of cooperation within the SCO Prime Minister Daniel Akhmetov of Kazakhstan stated that the plan would help develop a new energy network in the Asian region. Russia, Kazakhstan, Turkmenistan and Uzbekistan are the region's largest exporters of hydro-carbon resources. These states need a reliable energy market. The neighbouring China is the world's largest consumer projected to import 200 million tons of oil by 2010 and 250 million tons by 2020. Given the global growth of energy consumption, energy partnership is becoming the key area of international cooperation. SCO members can become a regular and stable source of energy supplies for China. Kazakhstan alone is expected to supply China 15-20 million tons of oil annually. An oil pipeline linking Kazakhstan with the Xinjiang province of China (Atasu-Alashankou) has already been completed. A complete overhaul of the Kyrgyz pipeline network is already in progress and a Russia-China pipeline project is under discussion.

The Chinese showed interest in developing the Caspian fields at the first SCO investment and development forum meeting held in 2002. China needs the Caspian region energy resources to meet its growing needs to sustain its rapidly growing economy. With 30,000 barrels a day moving to China via Atasu-Alashankou oil pipeline already functional, Sino-Kazakhstan energy relations have transformed the energy map of the region. For Kazakhstan this ensures diversification of outlets contributing towards greater freedom and autonomy. For China it is part of the drive to augment energy supplies from a source nearer home accessible through the overland route not vulnerable to the US Navy's aircraft carrier led battleships as it is the course for the Chinese oil supplies from the Persian Gulf and Sudan.[16]

China's energy diplomacy gained an important success when it concluded in April 2006 an agreement with Turkmenistan to build a pipeline for transporting gas. China agreed to buy 30 billion cubic meters of gas from Turkmenistan each year starting 2004. In the first phase the gas will be delivered via Uzbekistan and Kazakhstan to Urumqi in Xinjiang and beyond it to Shanghai. The volume of supplies will be increased up to 50 bcm by 2010. Niyazov was reported to have broken the stranglehold of Russian monopoly over its gas reserves by having a new option of marketing it in the East bypassing Moscow.

China's energy engagement with Central Asia is increasing rapidly through various agreements with Almaty, Tashkent and Ashgabat. It is estimated that in the near future from Kazakhstan alone 1 million barrels of oil per day (one-fifth of future imports) would be flowing to China. Beijing has also made a deal worth $4 billion to buy Petro-Kazakhstan. The Chinese state oil giant CNPC has also entered into an agreement with the Kazakhstan National Oil and Gas Company (KazmunaiGaz) for developing the Darkhan oil field in the Kazakh sector of the Caspian Sea. The Darkhan sector is believed to contain 480 million tons of oil reserves. In Turkmenistan out of 37 Chinese investment projects involving a total investment of $383 million, $221 million are in the oil and gas sector. A Chinese company is already exploiting oil and gas field in Western Turkmenistan with a capacity of 2.3 million tons of oil annually. America is concerned over China's increasing pressure in the energy sector in the Central Asian and Caspian region.

Beijing is also increasing its engagement with Iran in the energy sector and is trying to forge energy ties with Saudi Arabia, an American ally and a close partner. China's strong hold on the energy resources in Central Asia is also expected to facilitate its extension to the neighbouring West Asian region. To keep the Americans out who are largely guided by the market forces, the Chinese firms are willing to pay more to the Central Asian Republics. China's Petro-Kazakhstan deal has been viewed as revenge on Washington for blocking the Chinese acquisition of the UNOCAL.

Washington was believed to have pressurized Kazakhstan to delay the construction of the Atasu-Alashankou pipeline to China which is considered to be a rival to Baku-Ceyhan pipeline. Chinese leadership is reported to have told the Tashkent Summit of SCO in 2004 that Beijing had a plan to invest $ 4 billion in the Central Asian countries.[17] China also conveyed its intention to pay the full cost of about $1.5 billion for construction of a highway from China to Central Asia via Kyrgyzstan.

Despite a growing realization in Moscow and Beijing about the soundness of political and military grounds for cooperation against hegemonic policies of Washington, their misunderstandings on the energy issue have taken a long time to disappear. Russian preference for the Nakhodka route favouring Japan has not been appreciated in Beijing. However, by the time of president Putin's China visit in March 2006 there was greater appreciation of the advantages of energy cooperation between Russia and China while not closing the gap among them and even the American option.

China's stagnant energy production and fast growing consumption is likely to expand in the coming two decades.

China has become one of the world's largest purchasers of oil, natural gas and nuclear technology. Energy security has been always an important agenda item at the SCO summits with the Russian-Chinese leadership China's oil consumption is projected to grow to 15 billion barrels per day by 2030 from 7.4 billion barrels in 2006. In the case of natural gas it is expected to increase to 198 bcm from 49 bcm during the same period.[18]

Russia naturally fits all the parameters for supplying the growing energy needs of China. In September 2007 the Russian Industry and Energy Ministry approved a plan proposed by Gazprom to invest $100 billion through 2030 to create an integrated production, transportation and supply system involving over 200 bcm of natural gas in East Siberia and the Russian Far East.[19] Deputy Chairman of the Gazprom management A. Ananenkov informed in December 2007 that Russian natural gas sales to Asia-Pacific countries—especially China, Japan and South Korea—from Siberia and the Russian Far East could reach 50 bcm by 2007.[20]

During Putin's March 2006 visit to Beijing, the two governments signed four energy cooperation agreements envisaging collaboration in oil, gas, electricity and nuclear energy. In March 2007, President Hu signed several energy cooperation agreements with Russian energy partners worth billions of dollars. These agreements were similar to the agreements signed earlier in March 2006 between Russian and Chinese companies. In April 2006, Russia Began construction of a massive East-Siberia-Pacific Ocean (ESPO) oil pipeline at a cost of $11.5 billion. As per the present Russian plan, the ESPO pipe line connecting Irkuts in Baikal to Nakhodka on the Pacific coast will have a branch line linking China directly to Eastern Siberia.[21]

According to Russian plans the 21st century could well see an important eastward shift in the direction of Russian energy export routes. However, the actual Russian energy exports to China have remained at an amazingly low level. Russia share of China's oil imports was in 2006 about 11-12 percent which was even less than the oil supplied by the Persian Gulf countries to some more distant African countries.[22] According to a report by American specialist, Richard Weitz published in August 2008 as a work of the USA Government, the majority of crude oil (about 80%) was exported to China from Russia by Railway through Zabaikal-Manzhouli border oil reloading terminal on the Chita-Harbin-Vladivostok railroad.[23] Rail transport of oil is two-and-a-half to three times more expensive than through pipeline.

Richard Weitz refers to China's Chief Energy Planner Zhang Guobau complaining about the Russian approach to oil transportation issue. Guobau is reported to have said:

The Sino-Russian pipeline question is one step forward, two steps back. Today is cloudy with a chance for sun while tomorrow is sunny with a chance for clouds. One moment Russia is saying they have made a decision, the next saying that no decision has been made .... Even though there have been a lot of promises expressing Russia's interest in exporting natural gas to China, in truth no real progress has been made. As for Russian electricity exports ... during all the years we've been connected together, Russia has only sent a total of 1 billion kilowatt hours of electricity to China.[24]

In recent years cooperation in the sphere of energy among the SCO member states has gained a momentum. Certain targets for development have been put forth and some tasks have been resolved concretely. In this respect mention may be made of the growth of Russian and Chinese investments in the projects for exploration, extraction and refinement of oil and gas in Kazakhstan, Uzbekistan and Kyrgyzstan. An oil pipeline from Kazakhstan to the Chinese province of Xinjiang has been completed. Russian companies are participating in the construction of new hydro-electric projects in Kyrgyzstan and Tajikistan. A new direction in energy cooperation in SCO has been added through joint exploration and extraction of rich hydro-carbon reserves in Central Asia and the Caspian region. In the latter region according to specialists, 6-7 per cent of the proven world reserves of oil and 38 per cent o natural gas are located.

The SCO has real prospects for development and cooperation in the sphere of nuclear energy. In the near future China is planning to construct 10 new Atomic power stations. In this sphere the rich scientific technical potential of the member states, Russia in the first place, as well as the rich deposits of uranium in Central Asia, can be utilized. Kyrgyzstan, Tajikistan and Kazakhstan possess unique hydro-electric potential which is at present harnessed about only 10 per cent of the existing potential. The SCO is also working on the possibilities of cooperation in the field of alternative sources of power derived from sun and wind and reproduction of energy from agro-products, bio-mass, etc.

The SCO member states are also cooperating in developing new technology to economise consumption of energy through construction of new materials which reduce the volume of energy consumption. The council of heads of government of the SCO member states at its meeting held in October 2005 in Moscow again underscored the importance of cooperation in the field of energy. In November 2005 in the ancient city of Sian, the SCO Secretariat organized jointly with the UN Economic and Social Commission for Asia and the Pacific

Ocean, the Development Bank of China, the Boao Forum for Asia and the UNDP, the first Eurasian Economic Forum. This forum exchanged views on questions of ensuring energy security in Eurasia, coordination of the policies of member states, the need for deepening the dialogue between the countries of the region in the sphere of energy.

The Forum also came out with the idea of creation of a special platform for strengthening contacts between governments and scientific circles. The International Scientific and Practical Conference on the Energy Market in Central Asia held in Tashkent in December 2005 promoted by the SCO Secretariat as one more step towards formation of a common energy diplomacy, which was to work for mutually beneficial and acceptable economic and political decisions to ensure the regional energy security.[25]

The organizer of the Tashkent Conference Mrs. G.I. Karimova in her opening speech underscored the "comparatively geographical compactness of the macro-region providing low expenditure and supply of energy resources to the consumer on account of the side-by-side location of the countries producing energy and the countries consuming it". She also highlighted the "importance of political stability in this space to ensure safety and dependability of the transit routes".[26] In this context Karimova drew attention to the "topicality of the question of formation of a common energy policy based on balance of interests and creation of a unified space within the framework of the SCO".[27]

Since antiquity Central Asia has formed a single cultural and economic space linking the region with Russia on the one side and China and the Indian sub-continent on the other. On account of colonial interference in the 19th century a disruption was caused in this space. However, it is gratifying to note that this region has again reemerged as an important region in the global economy. At the Kabul Conference on Partnership, Trade and Development in Greater Central Asia in April 2006 the Foreign Minister of Kazakhstan K. Tokayev emphasized that the countries of the region are developing their transit capabilities, becoming suppliers of valuable goods to world markets such as oil and gas, mineral ores and agricultural products. We can already foresee outlines of new routes for oil and gas pipelines, roads and railways in the 21st century which more or less follow the routes of the Great Silk Road.

The SCO has great potential to act as a vehicle to promote development of infrastructure and economic cooperation in this region. The organization is poised to play a vital role in the joint struggle against drug-trafficking and international terrorism which is of crucial importance for maintaining stability and ensuring economic development in the region. As the SCO celebrated the five years of its existence on 15 June 2006, divergent opinions were expressed on the eve of this landmark event. The skeptics recalled the Sino-Soviet honeymoon of the 1950s and cited the absence of a common social base as a destabilizing factor for the growth of the SCO. It was stated that Russia was becoming more and more European with a large section of its population shifting to Russia's European part from its Far Eastern areas and Siberia. They also pointed out to the fear factor in the Sino-Russian relations as problems do exist in their bilateral relations.

However, the SCO has a more solid prospect of survival as it was based on pragmatism and balance of mutual interests replacing the old ideological romanticism. The SCO is a new type of regional organization with its accent on strengthening security as well as economic development through mutually beneficial relations based on mutual trust. On 14-16 June 2006 the SCO celebrated its fifth anniversary at its annual summit meeting in Shanghai the city of its founding. The meeting brought together not only the heads of states of the member countries but also of the observer nations—Mongolia, Iran and Pakistan (India was represented by its Oil and Natural Gas Minister Murli Deora). The member states together with the observers represented an overwhelming majority of world's population. Also present were representatives of the UN and members of the ASEAN. The President of Afghanistan participated as a special invitee. The US Defence Secretary Donald Rumsfeld, publicly expressed his resentment against the participation of the Iranian President whom Washington places next in line on its "regime change" targets list.

On the first day of the conference which was largely devoted to private meetings and discourse on the economic issues, representative of more than 500 enterprises were present. Contracts worth more than $2 billion were signed on the first day on the sideline of the conference. The contracts included a highway project linking Uzbekistan and Tajikistan, a cement plant in Kyrgyzstan, a hydro-electric power house in Kazakhstan and two high voltage power lines in Tajikistan.

China and other SCO members are presently working on 127 joint projects covering the areas of trade, investment, customs, finance, taxation, agriculture, technology, telecommunication, environment, health and education. At the Conference China committed $900 million in loan for projects in the region. At the Shanghai Summit the Kazakh President gave a call for revival of Silk Road. He underlined the importance of transportation links for the economic development of the region. The Russian President Vladimir Putin set the goal to "transform Central Asia into a dynamic part of the world economy'. Both presidents noted that the SCO would set-up an SCO banking consortium to coordinate financial arrangements among the regional nations.

The SCO has succeeded in establishing itself as a major institution contributing to stability and development in the area and shown its determination to establish new norms of international relations based on "Shanghai Spirit" featuring mutual trust, mutual benefit, equality, consultation, respect for multiculturalism and pursuit of common development.

The declaration signed at the Annual Summit called for discarding the Cold War mentality. At the forum President Hu Jintao proposed the formation of a convention featuring "lasting good neighbourhood relations and cooperation within the SCO framework'. The Chinese President appreciated the expansion of relations of the SCO with the countries of the CIS and other international organizations. Russian President Putin also emphasized the importance of understanding the cultural diversity in the region and greater efforts in the area of culture and education including the establishment of an SCO youth association.

The emergence of SCO as a full-fledged regional organization of a new type striving to bring stability and security to the vast Eurasian region on the basis of equal and mutually beneficial cooperation and inclusivity and openness is an encouraging development. This organization has, during its short period of existence, shown a particular potential to cope with the challenges of non-traditional threats to security in this part of the world. In many ways as this study has elaborated above, the SCO represents the successful culmination of the approach of peaceful co-existence and the Bandung Spirit jointly evolved by the two great Asian powers—India and China. It has also drawn heavily upon the Soviet approach to regional security in conformity with the principles of the UN Charter and international law.

As a new regional organization distancing itself from international power politics and focusing upon multi-dimensional cooperation among the regional actors the SCO deserves a serious attention from scholars studying the various constructive approaches to regional security. To say this, however, is not to ignore much less to brush under the carpet the threats and challenges which this young organization is faced with in the current situation.

While Chinese President Hu Jintao hailed the emergence o the SCO as an "important force" for peace and stability in the world, Russian President Vladimir Putin was cautious enough to acknowledge "growing competition" to a Moscow and Beijing led regional organisation encompassing Central Asia. Both Russia and China have repeatedly emphasized that the SCO was not designed to subvert the US interest in the region. At a meeting of the parliamentarians of the SCO states, where President Putin hinted at attempts to create competition to the SCO without naming the United States. The Speaker of the Russian Parliament, Gryzlov, made clear what Moscow had foremost in its mind while talking about competition. He posed the question, "Is it possible to fight terrorism and drug trafficking in the region without the participation of the region?" He regretted that the USA had a proposal to create in Central Asia an organization parallel to the SCO and observed, "This does not help the fight against threats. It only makes the threats bigger." [28]

Reports in the Russian and Chinese media have projected the "Greater Central Asian initiative' as a US plan to set-up a new grouping of Central Asian states, excluding Russia and China. The "Greater Central Asian initiative" which envisages the formation of a new grouping of five Central Asian states and Afghanistan under the US leadership as the main members with India and Pakistan also participating in it, is meant to promote "optional and flexible cooperation' in security, economy, democracy, transport and energy to make-up a new region combining Central and South Asia. As its leading advocate S. Frederick Starr wrote, "The United States is to shoulder the role of a midwife to promote the rebirth of entire region".[29]

The US Vice President Dick Cheney and Secretary of State Condoleezza Rice during their visit to Kazakhstan in 2005, tried actively to promote this idea. Entrenched in Afghanistan and Pakistan, Washington is dreaming of converting Afghanistan into a land bridge connecting the vast Kazakh steppes with the great parts of the Indian Ocean.

Although cooperation among members of the SCO continues to grow in various fields, it is yet to reach a substantial level particularly in the field of economic cooperation and trade. An undercurrent of suspicions and misgivings continues to act as a roadblock in the future development of the SCO. The perception of "yellow peril" is particularly strong in the Siberian and Far Eastern parts of Russia. Even in Central Asia there remains fear of a "creeping Chinese expansion", particularly in Kazakhstan and Kyrgyzstan which have a common border with China. Murat Auezov, a former Ambassador of Kazakhstan to China, is of the view that the Chinese have throughout their history attempted to expand their territories and continue to do the same.[30]

While some of the above mentioned old suspicions and misgivings remain in place to be overcome through forging of a high-level substantial economic cooperation among the SCO member states, the organization for the present seems poised for making slow but steady progress towards achievement of its professed objectives. The meeting of the Council of Heads of Government/Prime Ministers of Shanghai Cooperation Organisation in Dushanbe on 15 September 2006 can claim to have taken several important steps. The Dushanbe meeting was attended by the Prime Minister of China Wen Jiabao, Russia's Prime Minister Mikhail Fradkov, Kazakh, Prime Minister Danial Akhmetov and Kyrgyz Prime Minister Felix Kulov. Tajikistan was represented by its Prime Minister Ali Akilov and Uzbekistan by its Vice-Prime Minister Rustom Azimov. Besides them the other participants included representatives from the observer countries of the organisation, viz., Prime Minister of Pakistan Shaukat Aziz, Deputy Prime Minister of Mongolia M.N. Ethasian and Vice-President of Iran, Saidulo. The Vice President of Afghanistan Ahmed Jia Masood, participated as guest of the host party. The Secretary General of Eurasian Economic Community G. Rapota, SCO General Secretary Zhang Deguang and the Director the Executive Committee of the SCO Regional Anti-Terrorist Structure V. Kasimov also participated in the meeting. India was represented by Minister of State Prithviraj Chavan.

The meeting noted that since the previous October 2005 the Council of the meeting of Heads of Government in Moscow a considerable work had been done to boost trade, economic and cultural interaction among the six countries. It set out priority areas of cooperation for the coming period namely, energy, transport and telecommunication. The Heads of Government noted that the SCO economic cooperation had received new momentum following the foundation of the Business Council and SCO Inter Bank Association.

It also welcomed the legitimacy of the implementation of loans offered by China for joint projects and programmes in the SCO framework. It appreciated the work done by First Eurasian Economic Forum held in Xian in November 2005, the Trade and Industrial Forum in June 2006 and the Bishkek Economic Forum in Irkutsk (September 2006) which in its opinion helped to deepen economic interaction in the region. It was deemed useful to continue holding such forums in future as an important platform for exchanging opinions among government, business and financial circles of the SCO member states with an involvement of representatives of the business community from other interested countries.

The Council expressed satisfaction with the progressive development of people to people exchange including the 2005-06 plan adopted in July 2005 in Astana for a multilateral cultural cooperation among SCO member states. The 2007-08 plan on cultural cooperation was adopted in April 2006 in Tashkent. The signing on 15 June 2006 of the Agreement among the Government of SCO member states on cooperation in the area of education provided the legal framework for active joint efforts in this important long-term direction. The special working group on fuel and energy in interaction with the SCO Secretariat has been entrusted the task of studying in the shortest time the possibility of forming a "SCO Energy Club'.

To increase cooperation in the area of advanced information and telecommunication technology, the working group was asked to intensify its work on proposals about joint projects. The conclusion of the Memorandum on speeding up the work on agreeing and signing of the Draft Inter-Governmental Agreement on International Road Transport Facilitation is of particular significance. It urged upon the SCO Secretariat to intensify the process of negotiations to finalize the draft agreement.

The Dushanbe meeting of Heads of Government also considered the development of integration process to simplify and facilitate administrative and custom procedures related to international transit across the territories of the SCO member states. The Dushanbe meeting also drew attention to the creation of favourable investment climate in the SCO region. It also attached great importance to the first meeting of ministers in charge of environmental protection issued scheduled in Moscow.

The SCO Secretariat was charged with formulating a package of concrete measures on establishing interaction with the SCO observer states on economy and culture for their further consideration. It also recommended increased interaction with the Eurasian Economic Community (EurAsEc) based on memorandum of understanding between the SCO Secretariat and EurAsEc integration committee. The SCO Secretariat was charged with interaction, consultation and experience sharing practices in areas of mutual interest including economic, social, cultural and other fields.

The Dushanbe meeting of Heads of Government considered a number of pressing issues dealing with the organization's financial activity. It also adopted the SCO budget for 2006 and agreed to hold its next meeting in Tashkent. Certain developments in the field of cooperation among the SCO members in the energy sector and investment augur well for the future of this organization. The "Energy Club" proposal mooted out at the Dushanbe meeting, though such a club has not been officially established yet, is already perceived in the West as a prototype of "Eurasian Gas Opec".

Though the oil reserves of the SCO states are not of a great magnitude (they do not exceed 20 per cent of the World's total, together with Iran, which has an observer status), the case is different with gas. The total gas reserves of Russia, Central Asia and Iran exceed 50 per cent of the world known reserves. Iran has proposed to set gas prices and determine its major flow together with Russia which has startled the West.

Addressing the fifth meeting of SCO Prime Ministers, Wen Jiabao stated that the regional group had established multilevel mechanisms and channels for cooperation over the past several years. He also noted that factors such as the discrepancy in different members' legislation, and the unsatisfactory conditions of infrastructure, and capital supply had hampered economic exchanges. He proposed that the SCO members should strengthen coordination in legislation and policy making to create favourable conditions for trade and investment.

Highlighting the necessity of unified, transparent and fair rules for trade and investment as the basic requirement for regional economic cooperation, the Chinese leader suggested increased inter-parliamentary exchanges to improve coordination on legislation in the economic field. On infrastructure building, Wen proposed that the SCO members promote the construction of road transportation networks and information super highway projects. The region "should make use of its geographical advantage as the link between Asia and Europe for the development of cross-border transportation, and to connect telecommunication networks so as to create convenient channels for logistics and information flow" [31]— Wen Jiabao emphasized.

Highlighting the importance of Energy cooperation among the member states of SCO, Kazakhstan Prime Minister Akhmetov said, "I believe that in the future we will focus on issues related to energy security and I think this will be the pivotal challenge for our countries' economic development and implementation of this programme. An energy strategy and an energy club discussed at the SCO annual summit in Beijing are fundamental tasks of our government".

Similarly, Russian Premier mooted the idea of closer cooperation among member states in the energy related issues. He said, "It is important to ensure that SCO countries have mutual access to power grids, as well as improve the existing pipelines and build new gas shipment networks on their territory. Russian pipe producers are willing to take part in the project".[32]

In preparing the balance sheet of the SCO one cannot escape the fact that the organisation on account of its openness, inclusivity and accent on mutually beneficial cooperation on equal basis and its approach of strengthening regional security through non-military means stands apart as a unique trail blazing international organisation. The principles underlying it are unexceptionable as they are firmly grounded in the spirit of the UN Charter and fully conform with the universal norms and principles of international law. These principles are highly cherished by the people in India because of the wide popularity of the policy of non-alignment and Panchsheel.

Looking at the other side of practical achievements of the organisation in the field, one may come across with different opinion. While the skeptics may harp upon the multitude of contradictions between the two neighbouring great powers which have founded this organization, objective analysts cannot miss the positive contribution made by the SCO towards changing the scenario prevailing on the vast Eurasian landmass during the period of the Cold War and the Sino Soviet Schism. The Western strategists with their crazy, colonial geo-political ideas about the centrality of Eurasia for their global domination had conceived a satanic plan to turn this territory once known as a cradle of civilizations criss-crossed by the great Silk Route into a smouldering field of endless conflicts. The Shanghai Cooperation Organisation has reversed this process.

Besides, making a notable contribution to the fight against international terrorism, extremism and secessionism, the SCO has to its credit several other achievements, namely infrastructural development in the Central Asian and the adjoining Chinese territory of Xinjiang making the region as a important land bridge linking Europe with Asia. Thus SCO is making a significant contribution to this inter-continental connectivity by constructing railway lines, roads and oil and gas pipelines. The SCO through its meetings of the Heads of States and Governments, Foreign, Defence and Internal Security Ministers has taken active steps in the direction of coordinating the policies of the member states on vital problems and issues concerning the region and enhancement of its role in solving the global problems confronting the international community.

The Organization has particularly contributed in meeting the challenge of non-traditional threats to security from drug trafficking, illegal immigration and illicit traffic in arms. Its contribution to the fight against terrorism through anti-terrorist organization called RATS which is located at Tashkent is worth mentioning. The SCO has contributed in a big way to the training and equipment of security forces of the member countries. It has been instrumental in raising the level of their preparedness through organizing a number of military exercises. The organization has opened the RATS military exercises for interested outside countries as well. The SCO has come out with two conventions on counter terrorism. The first convention was signed at its founding summit in Shanghai in 2000. At the recently concluded summit in Yekaterinburg in

June 2009, another more comprehensive counter terrorism convention was signed by the member states.

In the opinion of the present writer much need not be made of the occasional changes in the foreign policy orientations of the Central Asian members of he organization. Some analysts in the West have perceived the developments between the SCO summits from 2005 to 2007 as giving an expression that the SCO was emerging as a powerful organization, successfully challenging American "hegemony". Shortly before the July 2005 summit in Astana, the US and other western governments criticized Uzbekistan for using force to suppress public demonstrations in the city of Andijan, whereupon the Uzbek President Islam Karimov asked the US forces stationed at the Khanabad base to leave within six months. At this summit held shortly thereafter, the SCO Presidents issued a joint declaration calling upon the US to fix a time table for pulling out all the military bases it had set up in Central Asia in the wake of 9/11. Washington did withdraw its forces from Uzbekistan and agreed to pay more to retain its base in Kyrgyzstan.

The SCO also added to its prestige and standing by granting India, Iran and Pakistan observer status in the organization. The 2006 SCO summit was attended by President Mahmoud Ahmedinejad of Iran (he also attended the later summits as well in 2007, 2008 and 2009) raising western apprehension of support by SCO of Tehran's confrontational approach towards the West. At the time of 2007 summit SCO military exercises took place in China leading to concerns in the West that there were plans to convert SCO into a military alliance.

But, the above anti-US policy orientation among Central Asian members of the SCO seems to be disappearing. Early 2008 witnessed the return of the US to Uzbekistan. But this happened not because of any problems in the Uzbek-Russian relations. Karimov started getting concerned over the deteriorating situation in neighbouring Afghanistan and thought it to be in his country's interest to patch up the differences with the US.

The SCO's record of progress in such fields as meeting the challenge of threat of terrorism and traffic in drugs on account of resurgence of the Taliban resistance to the international force in Afghanistan has been quite impressive in the post-2007 period considered by some analysts as marked by decline in Russian influence resulting in weakening of the organization. On the contrary this period has witnessed an increased interest in the affairs in Afghanistan by the SCO as is evident by convening of a special SCO Conference on Afghanistan in Moscow in March 2009. This conference made a notable contribution towards coordinating the anti-terrorist efforts of the SCO members by recommending several concrete measures for further strengthening the SCO counter-terrorist centre (RATS) based in Tashkent. The Moscow Conference (2009) suggested the participation of observer states as well as other interested states in the joint anti-terrorist military exercises conducted by the organization.

The SCO summits of Heads of States and Governments have during this recent period, made considerable contribution to development of cooperation in the field of energy, trade and infrastructure development. It further contributed to the development of a legal basis for fight against terrorism by signing a new comprehensive Counter-Terrorism Convention at the 2009 Conference in Yekaterinburg. The organization at its 2008 summit in Dushanbe came out with the innovative idea of having dialogue partners of the organization to overcome the problems it had been facing over its expansion by admitting new members. At the 2009 summit it agreed to have Sri Lanka and Belarus as dialogue partners. The addition of these two dialogue partners in creased the geographical limits of the organisation's jurisdiction to Europe and South Asia beyond the Eurasian landmass and its periphery.

The contribution made by the SCO in the post-2006 period since the completion of half a decade of its existence, in the field of development of concepts of security and regional cooperation, the conclusion of the Treaty on Long-Term Good-Neighbourliness, Friendship and Cooperation between Member States of the Shanghai Cooperation Organisation at Bishkek in 2007, stands out as a lodestar in the search for an ideal model of regional security and cooperation.

The SCO stands apart from its opposite model of security organization—NATO—in respect of generating new concepts and ideas having a great bearing on the vital issue facing the international community. The SCO member states deliberated seriously at their various fora over the on-going world economic crisis and the question of global security. These deliberations have culminated in the formulation of several constructive proposals which have attracted wide attention all over the world. Thus the world economic crisis was at the centre of attention at the October 2008 meeting of the Prime Ministers of the SCO member states held in Kazakhstan. At this meeting the Prime Minister of Russia, Vladimir Putin attributed the crisis to the "defectiveness of the monopoly in world finance and the policy of economic selfishness". He declared the intention of Russia "to take part in changing the global economic structure ... to guarantee stability and prosperity in the world and to ensure progress". Putin recommended the SCO model of "horizontal rather than vertical integration'. He pleaded for utilization by the SCO member states of the God-given "Competitive geographical and historical advantages" of the region.[33] He lauded the "principles and practice of complimentarity of avoiding inefficient and costly repetition and redundancy and what in the West is uncritically celebrated as 'competition'" which is characteristic of SCO.

Blaming the western policy of free liberalism for the present crisis, Putin said: "It is that precise variant of myopic and avaricious, ruthless and a social policy practiced over the past twenty years—when the US and its allies held practically uncontested sway over the world and were free to fashion it just as they chose to—that had led to the people of the West and the world steering into an economic and social abyss." A "qualitatively different geo-political situation" marked by "emergence of new centres of economic growth and political influence" was seen by Vladimir Putin as a redeeming feature.

As mentioned earlier the declaration adopted at the Yekaterinburg summit in June 2009 called on the member states of the organization to make efforts together with international community for the formation of a "more just, equal, all embracing and well regulated international financial regime which takes into account a true balance of interests of all its participants ...".[34]

On the question of global security too, the organization has established itself as a trail blazer breaking a new path. Emphasizing the non-military approach to security the SCO approach to security was outlined at the different summits particularly at the summit in Dushanbe in August 2008. The declaration adopted at this summit rejected "any attempt to strengthen a country's own security at the expanse of that of others" which was dubbed as "detrimental to maintaining global security and stability".[35]

As stated earlier, the SCO supports a comprehensive approach to security by taking into account "the interests of all parties involved and including them all in the negotiation process".[36] The overlapping of the Russian Sponsored Collective Security Treaty Organisation (CSTO) which does not include China among its members, and the SCO which has besides all the CSTO Central Asian member states both China and Russia has often been pointed out by critiques of the SCO as a sign of covert Sino-Russian rivalry over the common Eurasian space. However, there is not much substance in this criticism. In October 2007 the SCO and the CSTO signed a memorandum of mutual understanding to integrate regional and international security cooperation and the following month agreed as a collaborative approach on Afghanistan.[37]

The SCO which concluded its ninth summit in the Russian city of Yekatermburg in June 2009 may be rightly described as an institution and a concept with great potential. Its six full members constitute sixty percent of the territory of Eurasia with one third population of the world. If the Observer states are included it will cover half of the world population.

Former Joint Chief of Staff of the Russian Armed Forces and political analyst Leonid Ivashov thus described the significance and unique nature of the SCO: "Contrary to Samual Huntingtons Concept of the allegedly inevitable clash of civilizations, the conclusions drawn in the SCO framework was that harmonized interaction between civilizations and their mutual assistance were possible. The contours of an alliance of five non-western civilizations—Russian, Chinese, Muslim, Hindu and Buddhist—begin to materialize".[38]

That a regional security and cooperation organization like SCO comprising member states having widely divergent interests, orientations and aspirations, has acquired during a short span of eight years a credible stature in the international system is nothing short of a marvel. However, fortuitous developments arising out of numerous contradictions, at times give rise to a positive direction in history. The SCO is a case in point. One only hopes the pragmatic and transient considerations resulting in the emergence of a new regional security organization in Eurasia are strengthened further by objective factors. Such factors are likely to influence their overgrowth into a visionary model of international action for ensuring security with the efforts of the concerned nations of the region through equal and mutually beneficial cooperation and non-military means.

NOTES

1. "Meeting with Russian Journalists Following the Ceremonial Signing of Russia-Chinese Documents", Beijing, 21 March 2006, www.kremlin.ru
2. "Declaration on Establishment of Shanghai Cooperation Organisation", http://www.sectco.org/news-detail.asp?id=88&LanguageID=2
3. *Ibid.*
4. President Vladimir Putin in the Russian-Chinese Business Communities' Economic Forum, Beijing, 22 March 2006, www.mid.ru;
5. *Ibid.*
6. *Ibid.*
7. *Ibid.*
8. *China Perspective*, May-June, 2006, p. 32; "Sino-Russian Military Maneuvers: A Threat to U.S. Involvement in Eurasia", 30 September 2005, Heritage Institute Backgrounder".
9. *Ibid.*
10. *Ibid.*
11. Victor Litovkin, "SCO Military Tasks", *RIA-Novosti*, 11/05/2006
12. *Ibid.*
13. http://www.kommersant.com/page
14. "No Plans to Expand SCO—Russian Defense Minister", *RIA-Novosti*, 16/05/2006.
15. Irina Kulikova, "Economic Cooperation within the SCO", *RIA-Novosti*, 3/05/2006.

16. Girijesh Pant, "American Energy Policy in the Caspian Region: The Changing Energy Security Dynamics:, (Unpublished Project Paper), p. 15.
17. http://www.energybulletin.net/3193.html
18. See various reports by the EIA available on line at www.eia.doc.900/
19. *RIA-Novosti*, December 26, 2007
20. *RIA-Novosti*, December 24, 2007.
21. *Ibid.*
22. *RIA-Novosti*, December 27, 2007.
23. Richard Weitz, Russia-China Security Relations: Strategic Parallelism without Partnership or Passion, August 2008 p. 20; http://www.strategicinstitute.army.mil/
24. *World Politics Watch* March 29, 2007; www.worldpoliticswatch.com/article.aspx?id=669
25. Speech by D.M. Kulbaev, Deputy Secretary General of the SCO Secretariat, *Energorynok-Tsentranalnoi Tendencii i Perspektivy*, Tashkent, 2005, pp. 9-13.
26. *Energorynok-Tsentralnoi Tendencii i Perspektivy*, p. 7.
27. *Ibid.*
28. "Russia, China close ranks in Central Asia", Agence France Presse, 31/05/2006.
29. S. Fredric Starr, "A Partnership for Central Asia", *Foreign Affairs*, July-August 2005.
30. Rfe/Rl, 21.06.2006.
31. *China News*, 15/09/2006.
32. *RIA-Novosti*, 20/09/2006.
33. *Interfax*, October 30, 2008.
34. Yekaterinburg Declaration ... June 2009; http://www.sectsco.org/En/showasp?id=87
35. Dushanabe Declaration of the Heads of the Member States of the Shanghai Cooperation Organisation; http://www.sectsco.org/En/show.asp?id=90; see also, SCO leaders issue declaration on security and energy – Peoples' Daily online; http://English.Peoples'daily.com.cn/90001/90776/90883/6489033/html
36. Cited in Mark N. Katz, Russia and the Shanghai Cooperation Organisation, p. 12; http://www.eurasia.net.org/departments/insight/article/pp0903308/f shtml
37. *Ibid.*
38. Strategic Culture Foundation, January 8, 2008.

Appendix I

Shanghai Convention on Combating Terrorism, Separatism and Extremism

The Republic of Kazakhstan, the People's Republic of China, the Kyrgyz Republic, the Russian Federation, the Republic of Tajikistan, and the Republic of Uzbekistan (hereinafter referred to as "the Parties"), guided by the purposes and principles of the Charter of the United Nations concerning primarily the maintenance of international peace and security and the promotion of friendly relations and cooperation among States; aware of the fact that terrorism, separatism and extremism constitute a threat to international peace and security, the promotion of friendly relations among States asism, separatism and extremism, as defined in this Convention, regardless of their motives, cannot be justified under any circumstances, and that the perpetrators of such acts should be prosecuted under the law; believing that joint efforts by the Parties within the framework of this Convention are an effective form of combating terrorism, separatism and extremism, have agreed as follows:

Article 1

1. For the purposes of this Convention, the terms used in it shall have the following meaning:

(1) "terrorism" means:

(a) any act recognized as an offence in one of the treaties listed in the Annex to this Convention (hereinafter referred to as "the Annex") and as defined in this Treaty;

(b) other act intended to cause death or serious bodily injury to a civilian, or any other person not taking an active part in the hostilities in a situation of armed conflict or to cause major damage to any material facility, as well as to organize, plan, aid and abet such act, when the purpose of such act, by its nature or context, is to intimidate a population, violate public security or to compel public authorities or an international organization to do or to abstain from doing any act, and prosecuted in accordance with the national laws of the Parties;

(2) "separatism" means any act intended to violate territorial integrity of a State including by annexation of any part of its territory or to disintegrate a State, committed in a violent manner, as well as planning and preparing, and abetting such act, and subject to criminal prosecuting in accordance with the national laws of the Parties;

(3) "Extremism" is an act aimed at seizing or keeping power through the use of violence or changing violently the constitutional regime of a State, as well as a violent encroachment upon public security, including organization, for the above purposes, of illegal armed formations and participation in them, criminally prosecuted in conformity with the national laws of the Parties.

2. This Article shall not affect any international treaty or any national law of the Parties, provides or may provide for a broader application of the terms used in this Article.

Article 2

1. The Parties, in accordance with this Convention and other international obligations and with due regard for their national legislations, shall cooperate in the area of prevention, identification and suppression of acts referred to in Article 1 (1) of this Convention.
2. In their mutual relations, the Parties shall consider acts referred to in Article 1 (1) of this Convention as extraditable offences.
3. In the course of implementation of this Convention with regard to issues concerning extradition and legal assistance in criminal cases, the Parties shall cooperate in conformity with international treaties to which they are parties and national laws of the Parties.

Article 3

The Parties shall take such measures as can prove necessary, including, as appropriate, in the field of their domestic legislation, in order to ensure that in no circumstances acts referred to in Article 1 (1) of this Convention should be subject to acquittal based upon exclusively political, philosophical, ideological, racial, ethnic, religious or any other similar considerations and that they should entail punishment proportionate to their gravity.

Article 4

1. Within 60 days after the Depositary has been notified about the completion of internal procedures necessary for the entry into force of this Convention, a Party shall provide to the Depositary, through diplomatic channels, in writing a list of its central competent authorities responsible for the implementation of this Convention, and the Depositary shall transmit the above list to other Parties.
2. Neutral competent authorities of the Parties in charge of issues relating to implementation of the provisions of this Convention shall directly communicate and interact with each other.
3. In case of any amendments to the list of central competent authorities of a Party, that Party shall send an appropriate notification to the Depositary who shall inform the other Parties accordingly.

Article 5

Upon mutual consent, the Parties can hold consultations, exchange views and coordinate their positions on issues of combating acts referred to in Article 1 (1) of this Convention, including within international organisations and at international forums.

Article 6

In accordance with this Convention, the central competent authorities of the Parties shall cooperate and assist each other through:

1. Exchange of information;
2. Execution of requests concerning operational search actions;
3. Development and implementation of agreed measures to prevent, identify and suppress acts referred to in Article 1 (1)

of this Convention, as well as mutual information on the results of their implementation;

4. Implementation of measures to prevent, identify and suppress, in their territories, acts referred to in Article 1 (1) of this Convention, that are aimed against other Parties;
5. Implementation of measures to prevent, identify and suppress financing, supplies of weapons and ammunition or any other forms of assistance to any person and/or organization for the purpose of committing acts referred to in Article 1 (1) of this Convention;
6. Implementation of measures to prevent, identify, suppress, prohibit or put an end to the activities aimed at training individuals for the purpose of committing acts referred to in Article 1 (1) of this Convention;
7. Exchange of regulatory legal acts and information concerning practical implementation thereof;
8. Exchange of experience in the field of prevention, identification or suppression of acts referred to in Article 1 (1) of this Convention;
9. Various forms of training, retraining or upgrading of their experts;
10. Conclusion, upon mutual consent of the Parties, of agreements on other forms of cooperation, including, as appropriate, practical assistance in suppressing acts referred to in Article 1 (1) of this Convention and mitigating consequences thereof. Such agreements shall be formalized in appropriate protocols that shall form an integral part of this Convention.

Article 7

The central competent authorities of the Parties shall exchange information of mutual interest, inter alia, on:

1. Planned and committed acts referred to in Article 1 (1) of this Convention, as well as identified and suppressed attempts to commit them;
2. Preparations to commit acts referred to in Article 1 (1) of this Convention, aimed against heads of state or other statesmen, personnel of diplomatic missions, consular

services and international organisations, as well as other persons under international protection and participants in governmental visits, international and governmental political, sports and other events;

3. Organizations, groups and individuals preparing and/or committing acts referred to in Article 1 (1) of this Convention or otherwise participating in those acts, including their purposes, objectives, ties and other information;
4. Illicit manufacturing, procurement, storage, transfer, movement, sales or use of strong toxic, and poisonous substances, explosives, radioactive materials, weapons, explosive devices, firearms, ammunition, nuclear, chemical, biological or other types of weapons of mass destruction, as well as materials and equipment which can be used for their production, for the purpose of committing acts referred to in Article 1 (1) of this Convention;
5. Identified or suspected sources of financing of acts indicated in Article 1 (1) of this Convention;
6. Forms, methods and means of committing acts indicated in Article 1 (1) of this Convention.

Article 8

1. Cooperation among central competent authorities of the Parties within the framework of this Convention shall be carried out in a bilateral or multilateral format on the basis of a request for assistance as well as by way of providing information upon the initiative of the central competent authority of a Party.
2. Requests or information shall be forwarded in writing. In case of urgency, the requests or information can be transmitted orally but within 72 hours thereafter they should be confirmed in writing and with the use of technical means of text transmission, as necessary.

   If there are any doubts about the authenticity of a request or information or the contents thereof additional confirmation or clarification of the above documents can be requested.
3. The request should contain the following:

- the name of the requesting and requested central competent authorities;
- purposes of and grounds for the request;
- description of the contents of the assistance required;
- any other information which could be useful for a timely and appropriate execution of the request;
- degree of confidentiality, as necessary.

4. Requests or information transmitted in writing shall be signed by the head of the requesting central competent authority or his or her deputies or shall be certified by the official seal of that central competent authority.
5. Requests and documents transmitted therein, as well as information shall be provided by the central competent authority in one of the working languages mentioned in Article 15 of this Convention.

Article 9

1. The requested central competent authority shall take all necessary measures to ensure a prompt and most complete execution of the request and, within the shortest possible time, shall provide information on the results of its consideration.
2. The requesting central competent authority shall be notified, without delay, about the circumstances that prevent or significantly hamper the execution of a request.
3. If the execution of a request is outside the competence of the requested central competent authority that authority shall transmit the request to another central competent authority of its State, which has the competence to execute it and shall without delay notify the requesting central competent authority accordingly.
4. The requested central competent authority can request additional information which it considers necessary for the execution of the request.
5. Requests shall be executed on the basis of the legislation of the requested Party. Upon request by the requesting central competent authority, the legislation of the requesting Party may be applied if this does not contradict fundamental legal principles or international obligations of the requested Party.

6. Execution of a request can be postponed or denied completely or in part in case the requested central competent authority considers that its execution could prejudice the sovereignty, security, public order or other substantial interests of its State or that it contradicts the legislation or international obligations of the requested Party.
7. Execution of a request can be denied if the act in connection with which the request was made does not constitute an offence under the legislation of the requested Party.
8. If, in accordance with paragraph 6 or 7 of this Article, the execution of a request is denied in full or in part or if it is postponed, the requesting central competent authority shall be notified accordingly in writing.

Article 10

The Parties will conclude a separate agreement and will adopt other necessary documents in order to establish and provide for functioning of a Parties Regional Counter-terrorist Structure with the headquarters in Bishkek, the purpose of which would be to effectively combat the acts referred to in Article 1 (1) of this Convention.

Article 11

1. For the purposes of implementation of this Convention, central competent authorities of the Parties may establish emergency lines of communication and hold regular and extraordinary meetings.
2. For the purposes of implementation of the provisions of this Convention, the Parties may, as necessary, provide technical and material assistance to each other.
3. Materials, special means, facilities and technical equipment received by a Party on the basis of this Convention from another Party shall not be subject to transfer without a prior written consent of the providing Party.
4. Information about methods of conducting operational search activities, specifications of special forces and means and supporting materials used by central competent authorities of the Parties in order to provide assistance within the framework of this Convention, shall not be subject to disclosure.

Article 12

The central competent authorities of the Parties may conclude specific agreements among them governing modalities for the implementation of this Convention.

Article 13

1. Each Party shall assure the confidential nature of the information and documents received if they are sensitive or if the providing Party considers their disclosure undesirable. The degree of sensitiveness of such information and documents shall be determined by the providing Party.
2. Without a written consent of the providing Party, the information or response to the request received pursuant to this Convention, may not be used for purposes other than those for which they were requested or provided.
3. The information and documents received by a Party pursuant to this Convention from another Party shall not be transmitted without a prior written consent of the providing Party.

Article 14

Each Party shall bear independently the costs of the implementation of this Convention, unless otherwise agreed.

Article 15

The working languages to be used by the central competent authorities of the Parties in their cooperation within the framework of this Convention shall be Chinese and Russian.

Article 16

This Convention shall not limit the right of the Parties to conclude other international treaties on matters that constitute the subject of this Convention and do not contradict its purposes and object, nor shall it affect the rights and obligations of the Parties under other international treaties to which they are Parties.

Article 17

Any disputes, concerning interpretation or application of this Convention shall be settled through consultation and negotiation between the interested Parties.

Article 18

1. This Convention shall be deposited with the People's Republic of China. Official copies of this Convention shall be sent by the Depositary to other Parties in the course of 15 days after its signing.
2. This Convention shall enter into force on the thirtieth day following the receipt by the Depositary the last notification in writing from the Republic of Kazakhstan, the People's Republic of China, the Kyrgyz Republic, the Russian Federation, the Republic of Tajikistan, or the Republic of Uzbekistan informing it of the completion of national procedures necessary for this Convention to enter into force.

Article 19

1. Following the entry into force of this Convention other States may, subject to the consent of all the Parties, accede to it.
2. This Convention shall enter into force for each acceding State on the thirtieth day following the receipt by the Depositary of a notification in writing informing it of the completion of national procedures necessary for this Convention to enter into force. On this date, the acceding State shall become Party to this Convention.

Article 20

1. Amendments and additions may, subject to the consent of all Parties, be made to the text of this Convention, which shall be effected by Protocols being an integral part of this Convention.
2. Any Party may withdraw from this Convention by notifying in writing the Depositary of the decision 12 months prior to the date of anticipated withdrawal. The Depositary shall inform the other Parties of this intention within a 30-day period following the receipt of the notification of withdrawal.

Article 21

1. When forwarding to the Depositary its notification of the completion of internal procedures necessary for this Convention to enter into force, a Party which does not participate in one of the treaties enumerated in the Annex may declare that this Convention shall be applied to the Party with that treaty regarded as not included in the Annex. Such declaration shall cease to be effective after notifying the Depositary of the entry of that treaty into force for the Party.
2. When one of the treaties listed in the Annex ceases to be effective for a Party, the latter shall make a declaration as provided for in paragraph 1 of this Article.
3. The Annex may be supplemented by treaties that meet the following conditions: they are open for signature to all States; they entered into force; and they were ratified, accepted, approved or acceded to by at least three Parties to this Convention.
4. After the entry into force of this Convention, any Party may propose an amendment to the Annex. The proposal for amending the Annex shall be forwarded to the Depositary in written form. The Depositary shall notify all the proposals that meet the requirements of paragraph 3 of this Article to the other Parties and seek their views on whether the proposed amendment should be adopted.
5. The proposed amendment shall be considered adopted and shall come into force for all the Parties 180 days after the Depositary has circulated the proposed amendment, except when one-third of the Parties to this Convention inform in writing the Depositary of their objections to it.

Done at Shanghai, this 15th of June, 2001, in one original copy in the Chinese and Russian languages, both texts having equal validity.

Appendix II

Declaration on Establishment of Shanghai Cooperation Organisation

The heads of state of the Republic of Kazakhstan, the People's Republic of China, the Kyrgyz Republic, the Russian Federation, the Republic of Tajikistan and the Republic of Uzbekistan,

Highly appraise the positive role played by the "Shanghai Five", in the five years since its founding, in promoting and deepening mutual trust, relations of friendship and good-neighborliness among the member states, consolidating regional security and stability and facilitating common development;

Unanimously recognise that the founding and development of the "Shanghai Five" have conformed to the post cold-war historic trend that mankind aspires to peace and development, shown the great potentiality of peaceful and friendly coexistence, unity and cooperation realized through mutual respect and confidence by countries with different civilization backgrounds and traditional cultures;

Point out, in particular, that the two agreements signed by the five heads of state of the Republic of Kazakhstan, the People's Republic of China, the Kyrgyz Republic, the Russian Federation and the Republic of Tajikistan respectively in Shanghai in 1996 and in Moscow in 1997, on confidence-building in the military sphere in border areas and on mutual reduction of military forces in the border areas, and the summary documents signed during their meetings in Alma-Ata (1998), Bishkek (1999), Dushanbe (2000), have made important contributions to preserving regional and world peace, security and stability, greatly enriched contemporary diplomatic and regional cooperation practices and exerted extensive and positive influence in the international society;

Firmly believe that against a background of the rapid development of the process of political multipolarisation and information globalisation in the 21st century, it is conducive to the member states more effectively jointly making use of the opportunities and replying to the new challenges and threats;

And hereby solemnly declare:

1. The Republic of Kazakhstan, the People's Republic of China, the Kyrgyz Republic, the Russian Federation, the Republic of Tajikistan and the Republic of Uzbekistan have founded the Shanghai Cooperation Organisation (SCO).
2. The purposes of the SCO are: strengthening mutual trust and good-neighborly friendship among the member states; encouraging effective cooperation among the member states in political, economic and trade, scientific and technological, cultural, educational, energy, communications, environment and other fields; devoting themselves jointly to preserving and safeguarding regional peace, security and stability; and establishing a democratic, fair and rational new international political and economic order.
3. The SCO shall hold a formal meeting of heads of state of the member states a year, hold meetings of heads of government regularly; the meetings shall be held in rotation among the member states. With a view to expanding and strengthening cooperation in all fields, in addition to the established meeting mechanisms for the leaders of the relevant departments, new meeting mechanisms may be set up in accordance with circumstances, and permanent and temporary expert groups may be formed to study work plans and proposals for further developing cooperation.
4. The "Shanghai Spirit" formed during the "Shanghai Five" process, with "mutual trust, mutual benefit, equality, consultation, respect for multicivilisations, striving for common development" as its basic contents, has been precious treasure accumulated in the cooperation among the countries of the region in recent years. This spirit should be carried forward so that it will become the norm governing relations among the SCO member states in the new century.
5. The SCO member states shall abide strictly by the purposes and principles of the Charter of the United Nations, mutually respect independence, sovereignty and territorial integrity, not interfere in each other's internal affairs, not use or threaten to use force against each other, adhere to equality and mutual benefit, resolve all problems through mutual consultations and not seek unilateral military superiority in contiguous regions.

6. The SCO has been evolved on the basis of the two agreements signed respectively in 1996 in Shanghai and in 1997 in Moscow on confidence-building in the military sphere in the border areas and on mutual reduction of military forces in border areas. Its cooperation has been expanded to political, economic and trade, cultural, scientific and technological, and other areas. The principles embodied in the above-mentioned agreements have determined the basis of the mutual relations among the SCO member states.
7. The SCO adheres to the principle of non-alignment, does not target any other country or region, and is open to the outside. It is ready to develop various forms of dialogue, exchanges and cooperation with other countries, international and regional organisations. On the basis of consensus, it shall admit as its new members those countries which recognise the cooperation purposes and tasks within the framework of the organisation, the principles expounded in Article 6 of the this declaration and other articles, and whose joining will facilitate the realisation of cooperation.
8. The SCO sets special store by and makes all necessary efforts to ensure regional security. The member states will cooperate closely to implement the Shanghai Convention on Combating Terrorism, Separatism and Extremism, including setting up an Antiterrorist Center of the SCO in Bishkek. Moreover, relevant multilateral cooperation documents will be formulated to restrain illegal weapons and narcotics smuggling, illegal immigration and other criminal activities.
9. The SCO will make use of the huge potential and extensive opportunities in the mutually beneficial cooperation in economic and trade fields among its member states, strive to enhance further development of both bilateral and multilateral cooperation among the member states and plurality of this cooperation. For this purpose, a negotiating process on trade and investment facilitation will be initiated within the framework of the SCO to formulate an outline of long-term, multilateral economic and trade cooperation and relevant documents will be signed.
10. The SCO member states will strengthen their consultations and coordination of activities in regional and international affairs, support and cooperate with each other closely on

major international and regional issues, and jointly promote and consolidate peace and stability of the region and the world. In the current international situation, it is of particular significance to preserve global strategic balance and stability.

11. To coordinate the cooperation of the departments in charge of the SCO member states and organise their mutual collaboration, a National Coordinators Council of the SCO member states is hereby set up and foreign ministers of the SCO member states will approve the council's temporary rules to regulate its activities.

The heads of state instruct the National Coordinators Council, on the basis of this declaration and the documents signed by the heads of state of the "Shanghai Five", to start drafting the Charter of the Shanghai Cooperation Organisation which, among other things, shall clearly enunciate the purposes, goals and tasks of future cooperation of the SCO, the principle and procedures for the admission of new members, legal effect of the decisions made and the way to conduct mutual coordination with other international organisations. The document will be signed at the 2002 meeting of heads of state.

Summarising the past and looking forward into the future, the heads of state firmly believe that the founding of the SCO marks the entry into a brand new development phase for the cooperation of the member states. This is in conformity with the trend of the times, the realities of this region and the fundamental interests of the peoples of the member states.

June 15, 2001, Shanghai

Appendix III

Charter of the Shanghai Cooperation Organization

The People's Republic of China, the Republic of Kazakhstan, the Kyrgyz Republic, the Russian Federation, the Republic of Tajikistan and the Republic of Uzbekistan being the founding states of the Shanghai Cooperation Organization (hereinafter SCO or the Organization),

Based on historically established ties between their peoples;

Striving for further enhancement of comprehensive cooperation;

Desiring to jointly contribute to the strengthening of peace and ensuring of security and stability in the region in the environment of developing political multipolarity and economic and information globalization;

Being convinced that the establishment of SCO will facilitate more efficient common use of opening possibilities and counteracting new challenges and threats;

Considering that interaction within SCO will promote the realization of a huge potential of goodneighborliness, unity and cooperation between States and their peoples;

Proceeding from the spirit of mutual trust, mutual advantage, equality, mutual consultations, respect for cultural variety and aspiration for joint development that was clearly established at the meeting of heads of six States in 2001 in Shanghai;

Noting that the compliance with the principles set out in the Agreement between the People's Republic of China, the Republic of Kazakhstan, the Kyrgyz Republic, the Russian Federation and the Republic of Tajikistan on Strengthening Confidence in the Military Field in the Border Area of 26 April, 1996, and in the Agreement between the People's Republic of China, the Republic of Kazakhstan, the Kyrgyz Republic, the Russian Federation and the Republic of Tajikistan on Mutual Reductions of Armed Forces in the Border Area of 24 April, 1997, as well as in the documents signed at summits of heads of the People's Republic of China, the Republic of Kazakhstan, the Kyrgyz Republic, the Russian Federation, the Republic of Tajikistan and the Republic of Uzbekistan in the period from 1998 to 2001, has made an important contribution to the maintenance of peace, security and stability in the region and in the world;

Reaffirming our adherence to the goals and principles of the Charter of the United Nations, other commonly acknowledged principles and rules of international law related to the maintenance of international peace, security and the development of goodneighborly and friendly relations, as well as the cooperation between States;

Guided by the provisions of the Declaration on the Creation of the Shanghai Cooperation Organization of 15 June, 2001,

Have agreed as follows:

Article 1: Goals and Tasks

The main goals and tasks of SCO are:

- to strengthen mutual trust, friendship and goodneighborliness between the member States;
- to consolidate multidisciplinary cooperation in the maintenance and strengthening of peace, security and stability in the region and promotion of a new democratic, fair and rational political and economic international order;
- to jointly counteract terrorism, separatism and extremism in all their manifestations, to fight against illicit narcotics and arms trafficking and other types of criminal activity of a transnational character, and also illegal migration;
- to encourage the efficient regional cooperation in such spheres as politics, trade and economy, defense, law enforcement, environment protection, culture, science and technology, education, energy, transport, credit and finance, and also other spheres of common interest;
- to facilitate comprehensive and balanced economic growth, social and cultural development in the region through joint action on the basis of equal partnership for the purpose of a steady increase of living standards and improvement of living conditions of the peoples of the member States;
- to coordinate approaches to integration into the global economy;
- to promote human rights and fundamental freedoms in accordance with the international obligations of the member States and their national legislation;

- to maintain and develop relations with other States and international organizations;
- to cooperate in the prevention of international conflicts and in their peaceful settlement;
- to jointly search for solutions to the problems that would arise in the 21st century.

Article 2: Principles

The member States of SCO shall adhere to the following principles:

- mutual respect of sovereignty, independence, territorial integrity of States and inviolability of State borders, non-aggression, non-interference in internal affairs, non-use of force or threat of its use in international relations, seeking no unilateral military superiority in adjacent areas;
- equality of all member States, search of common positions on the basis of mutual understanding and respect for opinions of each of them;
- gradual implementation of joint activities in the spheres of mutual interest;
- peaceful settlement of disputes between the member States;
- SCO being not directed against other States and international organizations;
- prevention of any illegitimate acts directed against the SCO interests;
- implementation of obligations arising out of the present Charter and other documents adopted within the framework of SCO, in good faith.

Article 3: Areas of Cooperation

The main areas of cooperation within SCO shall be the following:

- maintenance of peace and enhancing security and confidence in the region;
- search of common positions on foreign policy issues of mutual interest, including issues arising within international organizations and international fora;
- development and implementation of measures aimed at jointly counteracting terrorism, separatism and extremism,

illicit narcotics and arms trafficking and other types of criminal activity of a transnational character, and also illegal migration;

- coordination of efforts in the field of disarmament and arms control;
- support for, and promotion of regional economic cooperation in various forms, fostering favourable environment for trade and investments with a view to gradually achieving free flow of goods, capitals, services and technologies;
- effective use of available transportation and communication infrastructure, improvement of transit capabilities of member States and development of energy systems;
- sound environmental management, including water resources management in the region, and implementation of particular joint environmental programs and projects;
- mutual assistance in preventing natural and man-made disasters and elimination of their implications;
- exchange of legal information in the interests of development of cooperation within SCO;
- development of interaction in such spheres as science and technology, education, health care, culture, sports and tourism.

The SCO member States may expand the spheres of cooperation by mutual agreement.

Article 4: Bodies

1. For the implementation of goals and objectives of the present Charter the following bodies shall operate within the Organization:
   - The Council of Heads of State;
   - The Council of Heads of Government (Prime Ministers);
   - The Council of Ministers of Foreign Affairs;
   - Meetings of Heads of Ministries and/or Agencies;
   - The Council of National Coordinators;
   - The Regional Counter-terrorist Structure;
   - Secretariat.
2. The functions and working procedures for the SCO bodies, other than the Regional Counter-terrorist Structure, shall be

governed by appropriate provisions adopted by the Council of Heads of State.

3. The Council of Heads of State may decide to establish other SCO bodies. New bodies shall be established by the adoption of additional protocols to the present Charter which enter into force in the procedure, set forth in Article 21 of this Charter.

Article 5: The Council of Heads of State

The Council of Heads of State shall be the supreme SCO body. It shall determine priorities and define major areas of activities of the Organization, decide upon the fundamental issues of its internal arrangement and functioning and its interaction with other States and international organizations, as well as consider the most topical international issues.

The Council shall hold its regular meetings once a year. A meeting of the Council of Heads of State shall be chaired by the head of State organizing this regular meeting. The venue of a regular meeting of the Council shall generally be determined in the Russian alphabetic order of names of the SCO member States.

Article 6: The Council of Heads of Government (Prime Ministers)

The Council of Heads of Government (Prime Ministers) shall approve the budget of the Organization, consider and decide upon major issues related to particular, especially economic, spheres of interaction within the Organization.

The Council shall hold its regular meetings once a year. A meeting of the Council shall be chaired by the head of Government (Prime Minister) of the State on whose territory the meeting takes place.

The venue of a regular meeting of the Council shall be determined by prior agreement among heads of Government (Prime Ministers) of the member States.

Article 7: The Council of Ministers of Foreign Affairs

The Council of Ministers of Foreign Affairs shall consider issues related to day-to-day activities of the Organization, preparation of meetings of the Council of Heads of State and holding of consultations on international problems within the Organization. The Council may, as appropriate, make statements on behalf of SCO.

The Council shall generally meet one month prior to a meeting of the Council of Heads of State. Extraordinary meetings of the Council of Ministers of Foreign Affairs shall be convened on the initiative of at least two member States and upon consent of ministers of foreign affairs of all other member States. The venue of a regular or extraordinary meeting of the Council shall be determined by mutual agreement.

The Council shall be chaired by the minister of foreign affairs of the member State on whose territory the regular meeting of the Council of Heads of State takes place, during the period starting from the date of the last ordinary meeting of the Council of Heads of State to the date of the next ordinary meeting of the Council of Heads of State.

The Chairman of the Council of Ministers of Foreign Affairs shall represent the Organization in its external contacts, in accordance with the Rules of Procedure of the Council.

Article 8: Meetings of Heads of Ministries and/or Agencies

According to decisions of the Council of Heads of State and the Council of Heads of Government (Prime Ministers) heads of branch ministries and/or agencies of the member States shall hold, on a regular basis, meetings for consideration of particular issues of interaction in respective fields within SCO.

A meeting shall be chaired by the head of a respective ministry and/or agency of the State organizing the meeting. The venue and date of a meeting shall be agreed upon in advance.

For the preparation and holding meetings the member States may, upon prior agreement, establish permanent or ad hoc working groups of experts which carry out their activities in accordance with the regulations adopted by the meetings of heads of ministries and/or agencies. These groups shall consist of representatives of ministries and/or agencies of the member States.

Article 9: The Council of National Coordinators

The Council of National Coordinators shall be a SCO body that coordinates and directs day-to-day activities of the Organization.

It shall make the necessary preparation for the meetings of the Council of Heads of State, the Council of Heads of Government (Prime Ministers) and the Council of Ministers of Foreign Affairs. National coordinators shall be appointed by each member State in accordance with its internal rules and procedures.

The Council shall hold its meetings at least three times a year. A meeting of the Council shall be chaired by the national coordinator of the member State on whose territory the regular meeting of the Council of Heads of State takes place, from the date of the last ordinary meeting of the Council of Heads of State to the date of the next ordinary meeting of the Council of Heads of State.

The Chairman of the Council of National Coordinators may on the instruction of the Chairman of the Council of Ministers of Foreign Affairs represent the Organization in its external contacts, in accordance with the Rules of Procedure of the Council of National Coordinators.

Article 10: Regional Counter-Terrorist Structure

The Regional Counter-terrorist Structure established by the member States of the Shanghai Convention to combat terrorism, separatism and extremism of 15 June, 2001, located in Bishkek, the Kyrgyz Republic, shall be a standing SCO body.

Its main objectives and functions, principles of its constitution and financing, as well as its rules of procedure shall be governed by a separate international treaty concluded by the member States, and other necessary instruments adopted by them.

Article 11: Secretariat

Secretariat shall be a standing SCO administrative body. It shall provide organizational and technical support to the activities carried out in the framework of SCO and prepare proposals on the annual budget of the Organization.

The Secretariat shall be headed by the Executive Secretary to be appointed by the Council of Heads of State on nomination by the Council of Ministers of Foreign Affairs.

The Executive Secretary shall be appointed from among the nationals of member States on a rotational basis in the Russian alphabetic order of the member States' names for a period of three years without a right to be reappointed for another period.

The Executive Secretary deputies shall be appointed by the Council of Ministers of Foreign Affairs on nomination by the Council of National Coordinators. They cannot be representatives of the State from which the Executive Secretary has been appointed.

The Secretariat officials shall be recruited from among nationals of the member States on a quota basis.

The Executive Secretary, his deputies and other Secretariat officials in fulfilling their official duties should not request or receive instructions from any member State and/or government, organization or physical persons. They should refrain from any actions that might affect their status as international officials reporting to SCO only.

The member States shall undertake to respect the international character of the duties of the Executive Secretary, his deputies and Secretariat staff and not to exert any influence upon them as they perform their official functions.

The SCO Secretariat shall be located at Beijing (the People's Republic of China).

Article 12: Financing

SCO shall have its own budget drawn up and executed in accordance with a special agreement between member States. This agreement shall also determine the amount of contributions paid annually by member States to the budget of the Organization on the basis of a cost-sharing principle.

Budgetary resources shall be used to finance standing SCO bodies in accordance with the above agreement. The member States shall cover themselves the expenses related to the participation of their representatives and experts in the activities of the Organization.

Article 13: Membership

The SCO membership shall be open for other States in the region that undertake to respect the objectives and principles of this Charter and to comply with the provisions of other international treaties and instruments adopted in the framework of SCO.

The admission of new members to SCO shall be decided upon by the Council of Heads of State on the basis of a representation made by the Council of Ministers of Foreign Affairs in response to an official request from the State concerned addressed to the acting Chairman of the Council of Ministers of Foreign Affairs.

SCO membership of a member State violating the provisions of this Charter and/or systematically failing to meet its obligations under international treaties and instruments, concluded in the framework of SCO, may be suspended by a decision of the Council of Heads of State adopted on the basis of a representation made by the Council of Ministers of Foreign Affairs. If this State goes on violating its obligations, the Council of Heads of State may take a decision to expel it from SCO as of the date fixed by the Council itself.

Any member State shall be entitled to withdraw from SCO by transmitting to the Depositary an official notification of its withdrawal from this Charter no later than twelve months before the date of withdrawal. The obligations arising from participation in this Charter and other instruments adopted within the framework of SCO shall be binding for the corresponding States until they are completely fulfilled.

Article 14: Relationship with Other States and International Organizations

SCO may interact and maintain dialogue, in particular in certain areas of cooperation, with other States and international organizations.

SCO may grant to the State or international organization concerned the status of a dialogue partner or observer. The rules and procedures for granting such a status shall be established by a special agreement of member States.

This Charter shall not affect the rights and obligations of the member States under other international treaties in which they participate.

Article 15: Legal Capacity

As a subject of international law, SCO shall have international legal capacity. It shall have such a legal capacity in the territory of each member State, which is required to achieve its goals and objectives.

SCO shall enjoy the rights of a legal person and may in particular:

- conclude treaties;
- acquire movable and immovable property and dispose of it;

- appear in court as litigant;
- open accounts and have monetary transactions made.

Article 16: Decisions-Taking Procedure

The SCO bodies shall take decisions by agreement without vote and their decisions shall be considered adopted if no member State has raised objections during the vote (consensus), except for the decisions on suspension of membership or expulsion from the Organization that shall be taken by "consensus minus one vote of the member State concerned"

Any member State may expose its opinion on particular aspects and/or concrete issues of the decisions taken which shall not be an obstacle to taking the decision as a whole. This opinion shall be placed on record.

Should one or several member States be not interested in implementing particular cooperation projects of interest to other member States, non-participation of the above said member States in these projects shall not prevent the implementation of such cooperation projects by the member States concerned and, at the same time, shall not prevent the said member States from joining such projects at a later stage.

Article 17: Implementation of Decisions

The decisions taken by the SCO bodies shall be implemented by the member States in accordance with the procedures set out in their national legislation.

Control of the compliance with obligations of the member States to implement this Charter, other agreements and decisions adopted within SCO shall be exercised by the SCO bodies within their competence.

Article 18: Permanent Representatives

In accordance with their domestic rules and procedures, the member States shall appoint their permanent representatives to the SCO Secretariat, which will be members of the diplomatic staff of the embassies of the member States in Beijing.

Article 19: Privileges and Immunities

SCO and its officials shall enjoy in the territories of all member States the privileges and immunities which are necessary for fulfilling functions and achieving goals of the Organization.

The volume of privileges and immunities of SCO and its officials shall be determined by a separate international treaty.

Article 20: Languages

The official and working languages of SCO shall be Russian and Chinese.

Article 21: Duration and Entry into Force

This Charter shall be of indefinite duration.

This Charter shall be subject to ratification by signatory States and shall enter into force on the thirtieth day following the date of the deposit of the fourth instrument of ratification.

For a State which signed this Charter and ratified it thereafter it shall enter into force on the date of the deposit of its instrument of ratification with the Depositary.

Upon its entering into force this Charter shall be open for acccssion by any State.

For each acceding State this Charter shall enter into force on the thirtieth day following the date of receiving by the Depositary of appropriate instruments of accession.

Article 22: Settlement of Disputes

In case of disputes or controversies arising out of interpretation or application of this Charter member States shall settle them through consultations and negotiations.

Article 23: Amendments and Additions

By mutual agreement of member States this Charter can be amended and supplemented. Decisions by the Council of Heads of State concerning amendments and additions shall be formalized by separate protocols which shall be its integral part and enter into force in accordance with the procedure provided for by Article 21 of this Charter.

Article 24: Reservations

No reservations can be made to this Charter which contradict the principles, goals and objectives of the Organization and could prevent any SCO body from performing its functions. If at least two thirds of member States have objections the reservations must be considered as contradicting the principles, goals and objectives of the Organization or preventing any body from performing its functions and being null and void.

Article 25: Depositary

The People's Republic of China shall be the Depositary of this Charter.

Article 26: Registration

Pursuant to Article 102 of the Charter of the United Nations, this Charter is subject to registration with the Secretariat of the United Nations.

Done at Saint-Petersburg the seventh day of June 2002 in a single original in the Chinese and Russian languages, both texts being equally authoritative.

The original copy of this Charter shall be deposited with the Depositary who will circulate its certified copies to all signatory States.

Appendix IV

Provisional Scheme for Mutual Relations between the Shanghai Cooperation Organization and Other International Organizations and States

During the period prior to entry into force of multilateral instruments governing the procedures for mutual relations between the SCO and other international organizations and States in accordance with the provisions of the SCO Charter the following provisional scheme for such relations shall be applied:

1. A non-member of the SCO and/or an international organization shall be invited, with the prior consent of all Member States, to participate in a plenary of the Foreign Ministers' Council as guests of the acting Chairman of the FMC. Such an invitation shall be preliminarily agreed upon though the Council of National Coordinators of the SCO Member States.

The invitation and provisional agenda of the meeting shall be sent by the foreign office headed by the acting Chairman of the FMC not later than one month prior to the date of the meeting. The invitation shall specify the procedure for participation in a FMC meeting as a guest. It shall also be indicated that in case the invitation is accepted the State and/or the international organization concerned should notify the FMC Chairman thereof not later than ten days prior to the date of the meeting.

A guest shall participate in a FMC meeting at a foreign minister's level. An international organization should be represented at a FMC meeting at a level not lower than the deputy head of the organization. The representatives of the SCO non-members or international organizations shall cover all the expenses related to their participation in a FMC meeting.

In case of an explicitly expressed desire to take the floor a guest may be given the floor subject to the established procedure and only when representatives of all SCO Member States will have spoken. The text of the address shall be put on record.

In case of an explicitly expressed desire by a guest copies of the texts of official documents adopted at a FMC meeting may be transmitted to such a guest.

A guest shall not be entitled to sign documents adopted at a FMC meeting, to propose amendments or additions to them, to put forward draft documents to be adopted by a FMC meeting.

A guest shall not take part in joint meetings of the ministers of foreign affairs of Member States with representatives of mass media on the outcome of a FMC meeting.

The invitation of a guest to a FMC meeting shall be valid for this meeting only and shall not imply an automatic invitation to subsequent FMC meetings.

Representatives of no more than two states and/or two international organizations may participate simultaneously as guests in a meeting.

2. A non-member of the SCO and/or an international organization shall be invited, with the prior consent of all Member States, to participate in multilateral consultations on political issues held by the ministries of foreign affairs of the SCO Member States. Such an invitation shall be preliminarily agreed upon through the Council of National Coordinators of the SCO Member States.

The invitation and the topic of the consultations shall be sent to the guest on behalf of the foreign office of the host country of the consultations not later than one month prior to the date of the consultations. The invitation shall specify the procedure for participation in the consultations as a guest. It shall also be indicated that in case the invitation is accepted the guest should notify the foreign office of the host country of the consultations thereof not later than ten days prior to the date of the consultations.

An invited non-member of the SCO and/or an international organization should be represented at the consultations at a level corresponding to that of the representatives of Member States of the SCO present at the consultations.

A guest may participate in the discussions during consultations, but shall not be entitled to sign final documents of the consultations and propose amendments or additions to them.

Copies of consultations' final documents may be transmitted to the guest.

The invitation of a guest to consultations shall be valid only for the consultations concerned and shall not imply an automatic invitation to subsequent consultations or consultations on other issues.

Representatives of no more than two states and/or international organizations may participate simultaneously as guests in consultations.

3. The SCO shall participate in the activities conducted under the aegis of other international organizations with prior consent of all Member States, at the level of the FMC acting Chairman or, on his instruction, at the level of the Chairman of the Council of National Coordinators of the SCO Member States.

Invitations should be addressed to the Chairman of the FMC on whose behalf necessary responses shall be given.

After receiving an invitation the Chairman of the FMC shall concert through the Council of National Coordinators of the SCO Member States various opinions concerning the form and procedure for SCO participation in a corresponding event, level and composition of its delegation as well as theses for a statement on behalf of the SCO (draft theses shall be prepared by the foreign office headed by the FMC acting Chairman). The delegation may include representatives of all Member States whose expenses shall be covered by their own states as well as the Executive Secretary of the SCO and/or his or her deputies, the Director of the Executive Committee of the Regional conterterrorist structure and/or his or her deputies.

Having summed up the outcome of his/her participation in the activities of other international organizations, the SCO representative shall transmit to all Member States, through the Council of International Coordinators, general information and possible proposals and shall inform them about documents he/she received and the documents that were adopted and distributed in the course of the said activities.

4. The FMC acting Chairman may submit, with the prior consent of all Member States, an application for SCO participation in the activities of other international organizations. Submission of the said application shall be preliminarily agreed upon through the Council of National Coordinators of the SCO Member States.

The procedure for preparation for the SCO participation in such activities shall be similar to the one specified in paragraph 3 of this Provisional Scheme.

This Provisional Scheme shall be applied as of the day of its signing.

Done in the City of Moscow on November 23, 2002, in one original copy in the Chinese and Russian languages to be deposited with the People's Republic of China, both texts of this Provisional Scheme being equally authentic.

Appendix V

Moscow Declartion of Heads of Member States of Shanghai Co-operation Organisation

The Heads of States participating in the Shanghai Cooperation Organisation (hereafter the SCO, or the Organisation)—the People's Republic of China, the Republic of Kazakhstan, the Kyrgyz Republic, the Russian Federation, the Republic of Tajikistan and the Republic of Uzbekistan—met in Moscow at a crucial point, when SCO is entering the period of completion of its organisational establishment and beginning to function as an independent factor of international affairs, and they state the following:

I

The course of events in the world demonstrates that the decision taken in Shanghai on June 15, 2001, to establish the Organisation was timely and that it is meeting the main trend of regional and world developments.

The SCO Charter signed in St. Petersburg on June 7, 2002, created a solid legal framework for the development of the Organisation and enabled it to become an important factor of ensuring regional peace and stability and promoting peace and development all over the world.

Having reviewed progress in accomplishing the task set by the last year's SCO summit, the task of the earliest possible startup of all the SCO mechanisms stipulated by the Charter, the Heads of States believe that a great deal of useful work has been done in that direction over the past period.

The Heads of States approved the draft regulatory documents on the operating procedures of SCO bodies, including permanent ones such as the Secretariat in Beijing and the SCO Regional Antiterrorist Structure (RATS) headquartered in Bishkek, and also on the establishment of the emblem and flag of the Organisation.

Upon submission by the Council of Foreign Ministers of the SCO member sates the decision was taken to endorse Zhang Deguang (People's Republic of China) as the SCO Secretary-General.

Procedures for the formation and execution of the budget of the Organisation were agreed, and the Heads of States signed an appropriate Agreement to that effect.

The Heads of States stress the need to provide for the beginning of the work of the SCO permanent bodies not later than January 1, 2004.

In this context it is important to provide for the timely entry into effect of the SCO Charter and the RATS Agreement and the adoption of the first budget of the Organisation at the meeting of the Council of the Heads of Government (Prime Ministers) scheduled to take place in China this coming autumn, and also the completion of work on the financial provisions and rules of the Organisation and the draft documents stipulated by the RATS Agreement during 2003.

It has also been found necessary to expedite the formation of the RATS Council to address questions arising from the RATS Agreement.

The Heads of States thought it advisable to instruct the Council of National Coordinators to carry on work to agree concrete questions of the startup of the SCO mechanisms, recruiting appropriate experts of the sides for the purpose.

II

The SCO aims to jointly promote relations of partnership on the great expanses uniting our countries on a broad agenda that would include cooperation in the political, trade, economic and humanitarian spheres and in countering present-day threats and challenges.

While taking a positive view of the process of institutionalisation and concretisation of substantive collaboration within SCO in various fields over the period since the St. Petersburg summit, the Heads of States draw attention to the need to ensure efficient cooperation between the foreign policy, defence and law enforcement establishments, emergency services, the ministries of foreign economic relations, transport and culture and other government structures.

The upcoming meeting of the Council of the Heads of Government (Prime Ministers) will have an important role to play. Preparations for the meeting are to help intensify the ongoing negotiating process on ways of creating favourable conditions for trade and investment and on completing the draft long-term Program of multilateral trade and economic cooperation in accordance with the

September 14, 2001 Memorandum concluded by the governments of the SCO member states.

The Heads of States stress the importance of invigorating contacts between the foreign policy establishments on topical matters of international affairs, including in the international organisations, primarily the UN.

The Heads of States reaffirm that SCO today, at the stage of its emergence and startup of its permanent bodies, is following the principle of openness in its readiness to establish contacts with other international organisations and nations regardless of their geographic location under the Provisional Scheme approved by the foreign ministers on November 23, 2002.

III

The Heads of States note that the present-day world with its diversity of political and economic systems is changing rapidly. What is changing is not just the political structure, but the entire international security system. It is necessary to formulate and implement a new security concept that is based on mutual trust, mutual benefit, equality and cooperation.

They reaffirm the need for observing and fulfilling the main goals and principles of the UN Charter and commonly recognised norms of the international law.

It is necessary to respect the civilisational diversity of humankind and promote its development. Different cultures should progress together, borrowing the best each of them has to offer, and strive for the common while leaving their differences aside.

It is important to contribute to the even-paced and sustainable growth of the world economy for the sake of achieving prosperity for all nations.

IV

The Heads of States note that recognition of the important role of the United Nations and the UN Security Council in addressing major international problems is of fundamental importance. The United Nations can and must be reformed to keep abreast of the fast changing world situation and with due regard primarily for the needs to find effective solutions to world political and security problems.

The SCO member states proceed from the assumption that one of the main areas of UN work should be pre-emptive measures to avert conflicts in accordance with the UN Charter and the norms of the international law.

The SCO member states believe that the UN should have an important role to play in the reconstruction of Iraq. One precondition of this country's transition to a life of peace and to the building of a prosperous democratic society is respect for the national interests and sovereign rights of the Iraqi people and concrete and effective aid on the part of the international community.

V

The SCO member states believe that no country in the world can ward off present-day terrorism, the drugs threat or other trans-border challenges at a time of the growing globalisation of political, economic and social processes. In this context the pressing need for broad collaboration among all countries both at the regional and at the global level and for a practical contribution of each nation towards the solution of these truly global problems is beyond doubt.

The SCO member states, recognising the transnational nature of today's terrorism and being in the forefront of the fight against its practical manifestations, are following a course of mutual cooperation and vigorous participation in the efforts of the world community in the struggle against terrorism, in particular, in stopping its financing channels. In this matter they assign an important role to close collaboration between the law enforcement agencies and secret services, and also the defence agencies of the SCO member states.

Along with promoting collaboration within the SCO, the member states of the Organisation intend to vigorously cooperate with the Counter-Terrorism Committee of the UN Security Council. They attach much importance to the early finalisation in the UN of the draft International Convention on Nuclear Terrorism and Comprehensive Convention Against International Terrorism.

At the same time the SCO member states consistently and invariably proceed from the assumption that the fight against terrorism should be waged on the basis of the norms and principles of the international law, and it may not be identified with the fight against any faith, individual countries or nationalities.

The problem of illegal trafficking in narcotics, psychotropic substances and precursors is becoming more and more alarming. It calls for the most effective measures on the part of the international community, not the least because drugs trafficking is one of the financial bulwarks of international terrorism. The SCO member states are making practical efforts to arrange for collaboration within the Organisation in fighting illegal trafficking in narcotics, psychotropic substances and precursors, and to this end will conclude an appropriate multilateral agreement before the end of 2003.

The goal of intensifying multilateral cooperation in countering the drugs threat arising from Afghanistan—a threat that is already acquiring global dimensions—is particularly acute today. In this context, the SCO members states believe it a timely measure that an international strategy for comprehensive neutralisation of the Afghan drugs threat be drawn up under the UN auspices and reiterate their firm commitment to close cooperation with the UN and other international organisations under the UN Drug Control Program.

The SCO member states voice support for the efforts of Afghanistan's transition government to stabilise the situation in the country. The SCO countries believe that the latest world developments should not detract from the efforts of the world community in favour of the economic reconstruction of Afghanistan.

The SCO member states are firmly convinced that success in the fight against present dangers depends in large measure on solutions to socio-economic problems, among them the eradication of poverty, mass unemployment, illiteracy and discrimination on the grounds of race, ethnicity or faith. The drafting under the aegis of the UN of a Global Strategy for Countering New Threats and Challenges seems to offer a key in the search for effective solutions to security problems.

VI

The SCO member states are convinced that the Organisation can and must make a tangible contribution to safe and sustainable development not just on its own expanses, but in the world as a whole. The SCO is ready to actively participate in building a regional security system that would equally respect the interests and approaches of all participants, and it will constructively cooperate with all nations and alliances in this major matter.

The SCO member states believe that at a time of globalisation the role of such factor as the maintenance and strengthening of strategic stability, including the problem of non-proliferation of weapons of mass destruction, far from diminishing, is, on the contrary, growing more important in many respects.

Today it is more important than ever to pool the efforts of the international community in a search for ways of jointly building a structure and architecture of international security for that 21st century that would be acceptable to all nations.

The SCO member states are confident that the imperative of collaborative actions in the face of common dangers will prevail in the world and that humankind will opt in favour of a democratic world order that would guarantee ongoing progress and equal security for all nations in the world.

Moscow, 29 May 2003

Appendix VI

Tashkent Declaration of Heads of Member States of Shanghai Cooperation Organization

The Heads of States participating in the Shanghai Cooperation Organization (hereafter the SCO, or Organization)—the Republic of Kazakhstan, the People's Republic of China, the Kyrgyz Republic, the Russian Federation, the Republic of Tajikistan and the Republic of Uzbekistan, assembling in Tashkent for the session of the Council of Heads of SCO Member States on June 17, 2004, state the following:

I

The Heads of States emphasized, that successes, achieved by the SCO from the moment of its establishment, and changes in the international situation test having noted the successful accomplishment of tasks on completion of the organizational establishment of the SCO, approved at the Moscow summit in July 2003, positively evaluated the work, carried out by the Council of Ministers of Foreign Affairs and the Council of National Coordinators.

The Heads of States expressed satisfaction over the timely launch of SCO permanent bodies—the Secretariat in Beijing and the Executive Committee of the Regional Antiterrorist Structure (RATS) in Tashkent and made note of the significant efforts of Chinese and Uzbek parties on creating appropriate conditions for their comprehensive functioning.

In October 2003 the RATS supervising body the Council began functioning. Concrete working plan has been developed in the RATS and a number of necessary legal documents have been adopted. Thus, necessary preconditions have been created for the effective functioning of the RATS, called to impart systematic and purposeful character to interactions within the SCO framework aimed at realization of the Shanghai Convention on combating terrorism, separatism and extremism.

The importance of uninterrupted maintenance of work of mechanism for financing SCO activity has been noted to provide qualitative and effective accomplishment of forthcoming tasks facing the SCO.

To strengthen the SCO in general, and to develop its economic component of fundamental importance is the long-term Program of multilateral trade and economic cooperation among SCO member states, approved by the Council of Heads of Government (Prime Ministers) in Beijing in September 2003. The document has not only pointed out common understanding of business partnership reference points, goals and tasks of six countries for the period of up to 2020, but also outlined ways and methods of their realization.

The Council of Ministers of Foreign Affairs is actively working. The Protocol on cooperation and coordination of activity among the Ministries of Foreign Affairs of six countries is expected to play an important role in coordination of positions of six countries on urgent issues of international life.

The Heads of States support the initiative of Republic of Uzbekistan on holding regular meetings of National Security Council Secretaries of member states of the Organization aimed at strengthening cooperation of corresponding national bodies in confronting new threats and calls.

The Heads of States emphasize, that in new conditions the Council of National Coordinators, relying on the SCO Secretariat, should focus attention not only on providing coherent functioning of the Organization, but also on elaboration of conceptual approaches to further development of the SCO.

At the stage of its establishment, adhering to the principle of openness, the SCO has already entered the international interaction as its authoritative and equitable participant. The SCO will follow this line henceforth. The Regulations on the observer status of the Shanghai Cooperation Organization adopted in Tashkent has become a new essential step in establishing and expanding the SCO's contacts with other international associations and states, regardless of their geographical position. The work will be continued on documents regulating other forms of international cooperation of the Organization, stipulated by the SCO Charter.

II

With completion of institutional establishment period, the SCO has entered a stage of developing full-scale cooperation of member states within the framework of the Organization. The Heads of States stand in favour of progressive structured movement forward in all directions, specified by the SCO Charter. Thus, the interaction should have both long-term reference points, and priorities for the near perspective. The aim of interaction consists of joint definition of interests, which unify six countries on the basis of respect of their individuality and sovereign rights.

The Agreement among member states of the Shanghai Cooperation Organization on combating the trafficking of illegal narcotics and psychotropic substances, signed in Tashkent, will be of great importance for multilateral activity within the SCO framework on counteracting transnational threats and calls. The Heads of States consider, that the course of implementing this Agreement should be in sight of the mechanism of National Security Councils Secretaries meetings, which could also organize activity on preparing complex program document on interaction within the SCO framework in struggle against new calls and threats, including trafficking of illegal weapons and ammunitions, explosive, asphyxiate, poisonous and radioactive substances, recruiting mercenaries.

Progressive economic development of the Central Asia region and contiguous states, as well as satisfaction of population's essential vital needs are guarantee of their stability and security.

In this connection, the Heads of States consider it necessary, that coordination of the Action Plan on realization of abovementioned Program of multilateral trade and economic cooperation is to be completed and four created expert groups are to be fully functional by to the next session of the Council of Heads of Government (Prime Ministers) in Bishkek in autumn of 2004. It is important to envisage such systematic steps, realization of which is supposed to lead to modern forms of trade and economic cooperation and to increase in goods turnover among our countries, harmonize respective standards and legal base, gradually create favourable conditions for free movement of goods, capitals, services and technologies.

Besides already adopted and planned measures on stimulating integration processes within the SCO framework, the Heads of States consider it timely to start the creation of SCO Development Fund and SCO Business Council and authorize the SCO Secretariat to provide for the preparation of corresponding documents on realization of these projects in possibly short time.

As a whole, while positively assessing development of cooperation in various areas for the period after the Moscow summit, the Heads of States pay attention to necessity of providing precision and effectiveness of interaction by the Ministries, responsible for external economic and foreign trade activity, transport, defense, culture, liquidation of emergency situations consequences, as well as among other structures of SCO member states. Thus, to increase effectiveness of activity of the institute of meetings of Heads of the ministries and departments, the speediest completion of development and adoption of legal norms of interaction, as well as timely fulfillment of the achieved agreements acquire special significance.

Matters of environmental protection, rational and effective utilization of water resources had to be included into the agenda of developing cooperation within the Organization's framework. Corresponding ministries and services, as well as scientific institutions could begin this year joint work to prepare SCO strategy in these areas.

III

The Heads of States are convinced, that further development and strengthening of the SCO—which is not a bloc organization and is based on principles of equal partnership, mutual respect, trust and openness correspond to the main tendencies of international development and will promote broadening the scope of international dialogue.

The SCO is ready to actively participate in constructive formation of new architecture of security, capable to consolidate wide international efforts on counteracting new calls and threats to global and regional stability. To achieve these goals, the SCO will cooperate with other states and international structures, first of all with the UNO, to contribute in to security and stability not only in the SCO region, but also in the world in general.

The Heads of States express great concern in connection with a new sharp splash of terrorism and extremism. Various countries and regions of the world are becoming terrorist targets. Terrorism is flexibly adapting to the situation, applying modern technical means, and ready to exploit in its interests any unsettled conflicts.

The global threat of terrorism should be confronted by the global system of counteraction with the United Nations as its central core, which should rely on regional, subregional and national structures.

Thus it is important to not only respond adequately to terrorist actions, but also to work on prevention.

SCO member states will strengthen cooperation in security field, with the purpose of increasing efficiency of struggle against terrorism, separatism and extremism and protecting their common interests. The Heads of States make note of the expediency of carrying out of joint antiterrorist exercises with the participation of law enforcement bodies and special services aimed at strengthening coordination in struggle against these threats.

The Heads of States believe, that answers to modern complex calls whether it is an international terrorism or regional conflicts and crises can and should be found on bases of multilateralism and cooperativeness without division of states into various categories, and with adherence of norms and principles of international law. Only such an approach will provide international security and stability in conditions of globalization. The SCO firmly intends to be guided by these principles in its activity and expresses readiness to actively cooperate with all states and multilateral associations on this conceptual basis.

Being interested in revival of peaceful, united and prospering Afghanistan, living in harmony with its neighbors and other countries of the world, the SCO welcomes formation of the wide-representative government in the country.

The SCO member states, recognizing the UNO's central coordinating role in implementing international programs in this country, will make efforts to promote international cooperation in struggle against terrorism, extremism and narcobusiness with the purpose to establish security, peace and tranquility, as well as create necessary conditions for peaceful reconstruction of Afghanistan.

IV

The Heads of States point out, that constructive cooperation of all regional associations in the Asia-Pacific region have determining importance for maintaining peace, stability and prosperity, which is, undoubtedly, in the interests of all countries located in the region.

The Heads of States address international organizations and forums functioning in the Asia-Pacific region with a proposal to start gradual creation of partnership network of multilateral associations by concluding among them corresponding agreements, including granting to each other on a mutual basis the observer status.

The Heads of States believe that realization of this initiative would promote formation in the Asia-Pacific region of cooperative system of common regional security and cooperation, acting within the framework of the UN Charter and international law, equally considering interests of all participants.

July 17, 2004, Tashkent

Appendix VII

Declaration of Heads of Member States of Shanghai Cooperation Organisation (Astana, July 05, 2005)

The heads of the member states of the Shanghai Cooperation Organisation—further mentioned as the SCO or the Organisation—of the Republic of Kazakhstan, the People's Republic of China, the Kyrgyz Republic, the Russian Federation, the Republic of Tajikistan and the Republic of Uzbekistan—having gathered at a meeting of the Council of Heads of SCO member states in Astana on July 05, 2005, state the following:

I

A year on, since the last meeting of heads of member states, the organization is becoming actively engaged in interaction with other international organisations and countries.

The SCO permanent bodies, which have been operating since 2004—Secretariat, based in Beijing, and Regional Anti-terrorist Structure (RATS) based in Tashkent,—are becoming effective collective instruments that provide an uninterrupted functioning of the Organisation. The RATS executive body—Council—has been playing a still more important role, which must increase further.

In order to enhance the effectiveness and coordination of the activity of the SCO and of all its bodies and mechanisms, the heads of the member states agreed that by their next high-level meeting in 2006 the Council of national coordinators will present proposals with regard to strengthening the role of Secretariat and renaming the Russian title of its chief as Secretary-General.

The heads of the member states underscored the importance of taking necessary measures on the fulfillment of agreements, which were reached at second meeting of secretaries of national security councils of SCO member states in Astana on June 02, 2005.

In order to contribute to the fulfillment by the RATS of the Shanghai Convention on combating terrorism, separatism and extremism, the heads of the member states agreed to set up an institution of permanent representatives of member states based upon the same principles, according to which permanent representatives of the member states to the Secretariat are now operating.

The heads of the member states express their confidence that the Concept of cooperation between SCO member states on combating terrorism, separatism and extremism, which has been adopted at the summit, will help enhance the effectiveness of such cooperation and make the activity of RATS more precise and targeted.

The heads of the member states assume that a meeting of the Council of heads of government (prime ministers), which is due in Moscow in autumn, 2005, will provide true momentum for the realisation of the Action Plan on fulfillment of the Program of multilateral trade and economic cooperation between SCO member states, for getting down to a more practical interaction between ministries and departments responsible for external trade and economic activity, transport, environmental protection, tackling of emergency situation, culture and education, as well as establish a rational financial and budgetary policy of the SCO.

The SCO Business Council, the formation of which is entering into a final stage, is to become a new source of stimulating the integration process within the framework of the Organisation. Guided by the principle of consensus, the parties will speed up the establishment of SCO Development Fund. At the same time the parties agreed to strengthen interaction between banks in order to provide financial support for the realisation of projects of regional cooperation.

While emphasizing a great and constructive job, which was done by the Council of ministers of foreign affairs, the heads of the member states underline the importance of a practical functioning of the already launched mechanism of consultations on international issues. They also consider the task of providing a well planned and targeted development of SCO external contacts an urgent one. Such issues should basically be handled by the Council of ministers of foreign affairs, and current coordination of external ties, being established by the SCO permanent bodies, should be done through the Council of national coordinators and in interaction with the Council of RATS.

The heads of the member states express their confidence that giving Pakistan, Iran and India observer status in the SCO will expand the Organisation's opportunities in terms of developing multilateral and mutually beneficial cooperation in various directions.

An important indication of the SCO's growing authority on the international stage is the obtaining by the Organisation of observer status at the UN General Assembly in December 2004 and the signing of memoranda of understanding between the SCO and CIS, the SCO and ASEAN.

In the immediate future the Council of national coordinators, jointly with the Secretariat and RATS, must work out a general approach so that the SCO could be able to develop contacts with the UN Secretariat, its commissions and committees and fulfill already signed documents on cooperation with other international organisations with maximum efficiency, as well as establish ties with regional associations, forums and interested countries built upon equality and mutual respect.

II

The heads of the member states point out that, against the backdrop of a contradictory process of globalisation, multilateral cooperation, which is based on the principles of equal right and mutual respect, non-intervention in internal affairs of sovereign states, non-confrontational way of thinking and consecutive . movement towards democratisation of international relations, contributes to overall peace and security, and call upon the international community, irrespective of its differences in ideology and social structure, to form a new concept of security based on mutual trust, mutual benefit, equality and interaction.

Diversity of cultures and civilisations in the world is a common human value. At a time of fast developing information technologies and communications it must stimulate mutual interest, tolerance, abandonment of extreme approaches and assessments, development of dialogue. Every people must be properly guaranteed *to* have *the* right to choose its own way of development.

The heads of the member states are convinced that a rational and just world order must be based upon consolidation of mutual trust and good-neighborly relations, upon the establishment of true partnership with no pretence to monopoly and domination in international affairs. Such order will become more stable and secure, if it comes to consider the supremacy of principles and standards of international law, before all, the UN Charter. In the area of human rights it is necessary to respect strictly and consecutively historical traditions and national features of every people, sovereign equality of all states.

The heads of the member states voice their support for rational and necessary reforms of the United Nations, aimed at enhancing the effectiveness and authority of this organisation. It was confirmed that, as the reforms got underway, it would be important to maintain as much broader consensus, to not impose any timeframe for the sake of overhauling the UN, as well as any voting on the projects, which are still causing a major disagreement.

The heads of the member states proceed from the assumption that in the 21st century the Asia Pacific region is destined to play an important part in providing peace and development, and declare against fault lines appearing both in the Asia Pacific region and in its separate constituent parts; declare for any misunderstanding and controversy among countries to be resolved by peaceful means and through negotiations; declare for an atmosphere of friendship, mutual understanding, interaction and constructiveness to come to reign in this dynamic region. Contributing to that is one of the main directions of the SCO activity.

The heads of the *member* states support the efforts by the Central Asian countries, aimed at providing peace, security and stability in their territory and in the whole region, and declare for the SCO to play an active role in strengthening stability and economic development in the Central Asia.

III

The heads of the member states believe that joint efforts by the member states are required in order to effectively confront new challenges and threats to security and stability in the region and in the world.

Such joint efforts must be of a complex nature and tangibly contribute to providing the territories, population, key objects of life support and infrastructure of the member states with a reliable protection from the destructive effect of new challenges and threats, to creating necessary conditions for steady development and elimination of poverty on the SCO terrain, and include the following:

- development of a close cooperation between diplomatic, foreign, external economic and law enforcement bodies, intelligence and defense agencies of the member states;

- active exploitation of the mechanism of meetings of secretaries of national security councils of the member states;
- formulation of effective measures and mechanisms of SCO joint reaction to situations, which threaten peace, security and stability in the region;
- joint planning and conduct of antiterrorist activities;
- harmonisation of national legislations on issues of security provision;
- cooperation on the invention and implementation of modern technical equipment used in fight against new challenges and threats;
- formation of an effective mechanism of mass media counteraction against new challenges and threats;
- training of respective personnel.

The SCO member states will prevent any attempts on their territories to prepare and commit acts of terror, including those aimed against the interests of other countries, not provide asylum for individuals, accused or suspected of conducting terrorist, separatist and extremist activity, and extradite such individuals at respective requests on the part of another SCO member state in strict accordance with the current legislation of the member states.

Measures will be taken to improve and enhance the effectiveness of the SCO Regional Antiterrorist Structure activity.

It is important that in the framework of fight against international terrorism the SCO solve problems, dealing with the liquidation of its material base, before all, through fighting illicit circulation of weapons, ammunition, explosives and drugs, transnational organised crime, illegal migration and mercenary activity. Special attention should be focused on preventing terrorists from misusing items of weapons of mass destruction, means of their delivery and on information terrorism.

Counter action against the financing of terrorism, separatism and extremism, including the legalisation of illegally made profits and money, urgently requires the formulation of united approaches and standards of monitoring money remittance, movement of financial resources of organisations and individuals, suspected of involvement in terrorism, as well as an active engagement by the SCO in respective international efforts.

In compliance with the Agreement on cooperation in the fight against illicit circulation of narcotic means, psychotropic substances and their precursors, signed on June 17, 2004, a matter of high priority must be the deepening of cooperation on tackling illicit circulation of narcotic means, psychotropic substances and their precursors. The SCO is ready to actively participate in the international efforts on the Formation of antinarcotic belts around Afghanistan, in formulation and realisation of special programs, providing assistance for Afghanistan in order to stabilise its social, economic and humanitarian situation.

We are supporting and shall continue to support the efforts by the international coalition, conducting anti-terrorist operation in Afghanistan. Today we are noticing the positive dynamics of stabilising internal political situation in Afghanistan. A number of the SCO member states provided their ground infrastructure for temporary stationing of military contingents of some states, members of the coalition, *as* well as their territory and air space for military transit in the interest of the antiterrorism operation.

Considering the completion of the active military stage of antiterrorist operation in Afghanistan, the member states of the Shanghai Cooperation Organisation consider it necessary, that respective members of the antiterrorist coalition set a final timeline for their temporary use of the above-mentioned objects of infrastructure and stay of their military contingents on the territories of the SCO member states.

Protection and development of key objects of infrastructure and transport are becoming ever more urgent in terms of preventing and tackling various kinds of technogenic disasters, consequences of which have aiready become an esseniial part of a set of threats to the new order. The SCO member states will work out multilateral mechanisms on a system of monitoring and exchange of analytical information in connection with possible disasters and their consequences, as well as on the creation of necessary iegai and organising conditions for conducting joint rescue operations, including education and training of personnel under united methods, its quick transfer and compatibility of technical means.

The SCO will be making a constructive contribution to the efforts by the wort: ' community on issues of providing security on land, at sea, in air space and inouter space in order to increase the fight potential of the member states of the Organisation for combating terrorism, separatism, extremism and other challenges and threats, the SCO member states will consecutively expand their cooperation in economic area, guided by the Program of multilateral tracts and economic cooperation and the Action Plan on its fulfillment, Practical steps will be taken in the field of ecology and rational use of natural resources.

Formulation of coordinated methods and recommendations on conducting prophylactic activities and respective explanatory work among the public in order to confront attempts of exerting a destructive influence on the public opinion is a vital task. The member states will actively contribute to the expansion of

interaction within the SCO framework in such areas as education, culture, sport and tourism.

The heads of the member states proceed from the assumption that joining efforts in the SCO framework for the purpose of providing security and expanding the Organisation's potential does not hurt the interests of other states and does not mean a movement towards the creation of any bloc, fully corresponds to the SCO principle of outside openness and the spirit of broad international interaction in confronting new challenges and threats.

President of the Republic of Kazakhstan
N. Nazarbaev

President of the People's Republic of China
Hu Jintao

Acting President of the Kyrgyz Republic
K. Bakiev

President of the Russian Federation
V. Putin

President of the Republic of Tajikistan
E. Rakhmonov

President of the Republic of Uzbekistan
I. Karimov

(*Astana, July 05, 2005*)

Appendix VIII

Joint Communiqué of Meeting of the Council of the Heads of the Member States of the Shanghai Cooperation Organisation, Shanghai 2006

On 15 June 2006, the Council of Heads of Member States of the Shanghai Cooperation Organisation (hereinafter referred to as the Organisation or the SCO) met in Shanghai, the People's Republic of China. The meeting was attended by President Nursultan Nazarbaev of the Republic of Kazakhstan, President Hu Jintao of the People's Republic of China, President Kurmanbek Bakiev of the Kyrgyz Republic, President Vladimir Putin of the Russian Federation, President Emomali Rakhmonov of the Republic of Tajikistan and President Islam Karimov of the Republic of Uzbekistan.

Secretary-General Zhang Deguang of the Organisation and Director Viacheslav Kasymov of the Executive Committee of the SCO Regional Antiterrorist Structure attended the meeting.

Representatives of the Observer States of the Organisation, namely, Shri Murli Deora, Minister of Petroleum and Natural Gas of the Republic of India, Mahmud Ahmadi-Nejad, President of the Islamic Republic of Iran, Nambaryn Enkhbayar, President of Mongolia, Pervez Musharraf, President of the Islamic Republic of Pakistan and Hamid Karzai, President of the Islamic Republic of Afghanistan, Vladimir Rushailo, Chairman of the Executive Committee of the Commonwealth of Independent States and Wilfrido V.Villacorta, Deputy Secretary-General of the Association of Southeast Asian Nations as guests of the host country participated in the meeting and made statements.

I

During the meeting, the heads of state signed the Declaration on the Fifth Anniversary of the Shanghai Cooperation Organisation and the Statement of Heads of Member States of Shanghai Cooperation Organisation On International Information Security, approved a new version of the regulations of the SCO Secretariat and a cooperation programme of SCO members on combating terrorism, separatism, extremism from 2007 to 2009, adopted a series of resolutions concerning personnel arrangement and the structure of the Organisation, and agreed that Mr. Bolat K. Nurgaliev (from Kazakhstan) will be the Secretary-General of the Organisation from 2007 to 2009.

The plenipotentiary representatives of member states of the Organisation signed an agreement on the procedure of organising and holding joint anti-terrorism actions in the territories of SCO member states, an agreement on identifying and severing infiltrating channels of people engaged in terrorism, separatism and extremism in the territories of SCO member states, an intergovernmental educational cooperation agreement of SCO member states, a resolution of the SCO Business Council, and an action plan of SCO Interbank Association member banks on supporting regional economic cooperation.

The heads of state met with the participants of the Inaugural Meeting of the SCO Business Council and attended the opening ceremony of the Art Festival of SCO member states.

In a constructive and cordial atmosphere, the Council of Heads of State summarised the achievements and experience of the Organisation in its growth, discussed pressing issues and tasks in the work of the SCO, and had an in-depth exchange of views on a wide range of international issues of common interest.

II

The heads of state pointed out that the Organisation has done a remarkable job in implementing the agreement reached in the Astana Summit held in the summer of 2005, and this has created favourable conditions for the Organisation to conduct more robust multilateral cooperation in various areas.

At the meeting of the Council of Heads of State, the Resolution on strengthening the role of the SCO Secretariat in the structure of the Organisation and changing the title of the head of the Secretariat into Secretary-General was adopted. This shall instill new vigor into the work of the Organisation and enhance the efficiency of the SCO's permanent body in fulfilling tasks of growing importance. In accordance with this principle, the Council of National Coordinators of SCO Member States shall hold consultation and make decision by the end of 2006 on the institutional reform of the SCO Secretariat and the rotation of staff for the SCO's permanent body in a way that ensures balance and the continuity of its work.

Having taken note of the fact that SCO member states have reached consensus on the principled position of formulating a mechanism for the Organisation to adopt measures in response to developments that threaten regional peace, stability and security, the heads of state believed that the SCO Secretariat should draft the relevant agreement as soon as possible, to ensure that all measures under the mechanism are law-based.

It remains the top priority of the Organisation to combat the threats posed by terrorism, separatism and extremism as well as illegal drug trafficking, which have not diminished but aggravated in scale and degree. Various forms of joint anti-terrorism military exercises within the territories of the SCO member states involving, among others, their defense authorities, will help enhance the efficiency of member states' joint anti-terrorism operations. The heads of state spoke positively of the work done by the SCO Regional Antiterrorist Structure, and were convinced that this Structure has the potential to better perform its duties and carry out its mission.

The heads of state pointed out that there is already a legal basis and an organisational structure for carrying out economic cooperation. The implementation of the Programme of Multilateral Economic and Trade Cooperation among SCO Member States and its Action Plan has begun. To establish the SCO Business Council and the Interbank Association will greatly enhance the development of economic cooperation of the Organisation. The credit fund of US$ 900 million provided by China will help expand regional cooperation. All member states agreed to give priority to cooperation in the fields of energy, information technology and transportation, which have entered the phase of carrying out pilot projects and is of special significance for deepening economic cooperation within the SCO framework.

The heads of state expressed their satisfaction with the progress made in areas of multilateral cooperation, i.e. environmental protection, culture, education and sports. They were also happy to see that the SCO Forum had begun functioning. The heads of state emphasised that the progress would be increasingly significant for enhancing mutual understanding among member states and conducting non-governmental exchanges within the SCO framework.

The heads of state expressed full support for the agreement (the SCO Parliamentary Initiative) signed at the Meeting of Parliament Speakers of SCO Member States held in Moscow on 30 May 2006, believing that the agreement is a good innovating action to consolidate the Organisation and develop the interparliamentary relations among the member states.

The heads of state considered that as the international situation evolves and the SCO becomes more dynamic, it is necessary to strengthen the Organisation's public information so as to create a public opinion favourable for its development. The SCO Secretariat should coordinate the drafting of specific proposals on this matter.

Threats of a military-political, criminal or terrorist nature to information security constitute common challenges for all member states that need to be dealt with through prompt joint measures. The experts' panel was entrusted with the task of producing a long-term plan of action for the maintenance of information security before the next Summit in 2007, including ways of solving this problem within the SCO framework.

In light of the SCO's lofty purposes and long-term interests and in pursuance of the declaration on the fifth anniversary of the SCO, the heads of state instructed the Council of National Coordinators to conduct consultations on concluding a multilateral legal document on long-term neighborly and amicable cooperation within the SCO framework.

III

The SCO will try to expand cooperation among member states in the international arena in various forms and by various means. It will hold regular consultations with observers and international organisations concerned. This is fully applicable to the SCO-Afghanistan Contact Group which is already functioning.

The heads of state pointed out with satisfaction that the initiative endorsed by the Council of Heads of State in Tashkent 2004 on establishing cooperative relations among international organisations in the Asia Pacific was warmly and widely received. They welcomed the signing of cooperation documents between the SCO and the Association of Southeast Asian Nations (ASEAN), the Commonwealth of Independent States (CIS) and the Eurasian Economic Community (EurAsEC). They reiterated that the SCO is ready to forge similar ties with other international organisations and financial institutions on the basis of equality and mutual respect.

The SCO Secretariat should, together with the Executive Committee of the SCO Regional Antiterrorist Structure, closely follow the implementation of cooperation documents signed between the SCO and other organisations and energetically promote concrete cooperation with the observers.

The heads of state also entrusted the Council of National Coordinators to make recommendations on the procedure of SCO membership enlargement. This procedure should fully conform to the purposes and goals set forth in the Charter of the Shanghai Cooperation Organisation, ensure the effectiveness of all treaties that form the legal basis of the SCO, help strengthen its unity and guarantee the applicability of the principle of consensus to consultations on all matters and at all levels of SCO.

The next meeting of the Council of Heads of State will be held in Bishkek in 2007. The Kyrgyz Republic will assume the SCO presidency next year.

Appendix IX

Bishkek Declaration of the Heads of the Member States of the Shanghai Cooperation Organisation

The heads of the member states of the Shanghai Cooperation Organisation (hereinafter referred to as the SCO or the Organisation)—the Republic of Kazakhstan, the People's Republic of China, the Kyrgyz Republic, the Russian Federation, the Republic of Tajikistan and the Republic of Uzbekistan, guided by united or similar approaches to the key problems of modernity, during a meeting of the Council of Heads of SCO Member States on 16 August 2007 in Bishkek state as follows:

The fast evolving process of globalisation adds to the interdependence of states, as a result their security and development become interconnected. Modern challenges and threats can be effectively counteracted through concerted efforts of the international community on the basis of agreed principles and in the framework of multilateral mechanisms. Unilateral action cannot resolve the existing problems.

An effective global security system can only be built under the auspices of the UN and in strict accordance with its Charter.

Cooperation in counteracting new challenges and threats must be conducted in a consistent manner, without resorting to double standards, in strict observance of norms of the international law.

The international security agenda must not exclude such tasks as ensuring the stability of world economy, reduction of poverty, evening up the social and economic development level, maintaining the economic, environmental, energy, informational security, as well as protection of the population and territories of the member states of the Organisation against natural and technological disasters.

The SCO member states advocate creation of a security structure on the basis of generally accepted norms of the international law that will:

- reflect the balance of interests of all subjects of international relations;
- guarantee the right of every state to choose independently its way of development based on its unique historical experience

and national features, to protect its state integrity and national dignity, to participate equally in international affairs;

- ensure the settlement of international and regional conflicts and crises through political and diplomatic means in strict accordance with principles and norms of the international law and with consideration of legitimate interests of all parties concerned;
- preserve the diversity of cultures and civilisations, encourage implementation of initiatives aimed at deepening of dialogue among civilisations and religions.

The SCO member states are determined to interact closely on tackling the issues of the UN reform. The reform of the pan global organisation, first and foremost its Security Council, must gain as much wider consensus of its members. Successful cooperation in this field is a key to genuine realisation of the aspiration of all the SCO member states towards comprehensive strengthening of the authority of the UN and reaffirming the central position of the Security Council in the field of protecting international peace and security.

The SCO member states consistently stand up for strengthening strategic stability, non-proliferation of weapons of mass destruction, and consider it an important and urgent step to draft an international legal document on preventing the deployment of weapons in outer space, use of force or the threat of using force against space objects.

The heads of state note the significance of approval of the Central Asia Nuclear-Weapon-Free Zone Treaty (Semipalatinsk, 8 September 2006) and welcome the adoption of the respective resolution at the 61st session of the UN General Assembly, which highly values the contribution of Central Asian states to the cause of consolidating the regime of nuclear non-proliferation, advancing cooperation on peaceful use of nuclear energy, as well as strengthening the international and regional peace and security.

The heads of state support the efforts of the participating states of the Central Asia Nuclear-Weapon-Free Zone Treaty on concluding a Protocol on Security Guarantees with the nuclear-weapon states, which would ensure genuine existence of a nuclear free zone in the region.

Being aware of the stimulating effect the rapid development and massive use of information technology is having on the social progress of humanity, the SCO member states express concern over the threat of using it for purposes inconsistent with the tasks of protecting international stability and security.

The SCO member states stand ready to develop cooperation and step up joint efforts on strengthening international information security in all aspects.

The heads of state believe that stability and security in Central Asia can be provided first and foremost by the forces of the region's states on the basis of international organisations already established in the region.

The member states stress the need for collective efforts on counteracting new challenges and threats. They highly rate the activity of the SCO Regional Antiterrorist Structure and believe that it possesses a significant potential for further enhancement of interaction in the fight against terrorism, separatism and extremism.

Expressing concern over the threat of narcotics coming from Afghanistan and its negative effect on Central Asia, the heads of state call for consistent strengthening of anti-narcotics cooperation in the framework of the Organisation, combining international efforts on the creation of anti-narcotics belts around Afghanistan. The SCO member states stand ready to participate in the efforts to normalise the political situation in Afghanistan, to develop economic cooperation with the country. The activity of the SCO—Afghanistan Contact Group will intensify.

The heads of the SCO member states note the important role of energy sector as a basis for steady economic growth and security, and attach special significance to strengthening interaction in this direction. Reliable and mutually beneficial partnership in various fields of energy sector will help strengthen the security and stability across the SCO region and the wider world alike. Comparison of energy strategies in the SCO framework is a pressing task. Considering the current resources, demand, capabilities and the potential, the SCO member states will continue to promote dialogue on energy issues and practical cooperation among energy-producing, transit and consumer states.

The SCO member states reaffirm their commitment to provide mutual practical assistance in implementation of the national economic development programmes.

The SCO member states reiterate that the Organisation is open for interaction with all interested partners based on the international law and generally accepted norms of international relations with the aim of finding mutually acceptable solutions for the pressing problems of modernity.

Appendix X

Treaty on Long-Term Good-Neighborliness, Friendship and Cooperation Between the Member States of the Shanghai Cooperation Organization

Member States of the Shanghai Cooperation Organization (hereinafter referred to as "the SCO", or "Organization"): the Republic of Kazakhstan, the People's Republic of China, the Kyrgyz Republic, the Russian Federation, the Republic of Tajikistan, the Republic of Uzbekistan, hereinafter referred to as "the Contracting Parties";

Bound by historical ties of good-neighborliness, friendship and cooperation;

Guided by the goals and principles of the Charter of the United Nations, universally recognized principles and norms of international law, as well as by the Charter of the Shanghai Cooperation Organization of 7 June 2002;

Convinced that strengthening and deepening relations of good-neighborliness, friendship and cooperation between the Member States of the Organization corresponds to the fundamental interests of their peoples and contributes to peace and development in the SCO space and in the whole world;

Recognizing that globalization processes increase interdependence of States, as a result of which their security and prosperity are becoming inextricably intertwined;

Believing that contemporary challenges and threats to security have a global nature and can only be effectively met through joint efforts and adherence to the agreed principles and interaction mechanisms;

Mindful of the need to respect cultural and civilizational variety of the contemporary world;

Reaffirming their readiness to expand mutually beneficial cooperation between them and with all interested States and international organizations to promote a just and rational world order creating favourable conditions for a sustainable development of the Organization's Member States;

Reaffirming further that this Treaty shall not be directed against any States or organizations, and that the Contracting Parties shall follow the principle of openness to the other countries of the world;

Seeking to make the SCO space a region of peace, cooperation, prosperity and harmony;

Guided by the intention to contribute to more democratic international relations and to the establishment of a new architecture of global security on the basis of equality, mutual respect, mutual trust and benefit, as well as abrogation of a bloc-based and ideological division;

Determined to strengthen friendly relations between the Organization's Member States so that friendship between their peoples is handed down from generation to generation;

Have agreed as follows:

Article 1

The Contracting Parties shall develop long-term relations of good-neighborliness, friendship and cooperation in the areas of mutual interest for the Contracting Parties in accordance with universally recognized principles and norms of international law.

Article 2

The Contracting Parties shall settle differences between them peacefully, using, as a guidance, the Charter of the United Nations and universally recognized principles and norms of international law, as well as the Charter of the Shanghai Cooperation Organization of 7 June 2002.

Article 3

The Contracting Parties shall respect each other's right to choose ways of political, economic, social and cultural development, taking into account the historical background and national peculiarities of each State.

Article 4

The Contracting Parties, respecting principles of state sovereignty and territorial integrity, shall take measures to prevent on their territories any activity incompatible with these principles.

The Contracting Parties shall not participate in alliances or organizations directed against other Contracting Parties and shall not support any actions hostile to other Contracting Parties.

Article 5

The Contracting Parties shall respect the principle of inviolability of borders and make active efforts to build confidence in border regions in the military sphere, determined to make the borders with each other borders of eternal peace and friendship.

Article 6

In case of a situation threatening its security, a Contracting Party may hold consultations within the Organization with other Contracting Parties to provide an adequate response to the situation that emerged.

Article 7

The Contracting Parties shall make efforts within the framework of the SCO to maintain and strengthen international peace and security, and shall promote coordination and cooperation in such areas as safeguarding and strengthening the role of the United Nations, maintaining global and regional stability, advancing international arms control process, preventing the proliferation of weapons of mass destruction and their delivery means; they shall also hold regular consultations on those issues.

Article 8

The Contracting Parties, in accordance with their national legislations and on the basis of observing generally recognized principles and norms of international law, international treaties, to which they are parties, shall actively develop cooperation to counteract terrorism, separatism and extremism; illegal trafficking in drugs, psychotropic substances and their precursors and arms; other forms of transnational criminal activity; as well as illegal migration.

The Contracting Parties, in accordance with their national legislations and on the basis of international treaties, to which they are parties, shall build up their interaction in searching, apprehending, extraditing and transferring persons suspected of, charged with or sentenced for committing crimes related to terrorist, separatist, extremist activities or other crimes.

The Contracting Parties shall develop cooperation in the field of state border security and customs control, regulation of labour migration, and provision of financial and information security.

Article 9

The Contracting Parties shall promote contacts and cooperation between law enforcement and judicial authorities of the Contracting Parties.

Article 10

The Contracting Parties shall develop various forms of cooperation between their Defense Ministries.

Article 11

The Contracting Parties shall develop cooperation in such fields as promoting the implementation of human rights and fundamental freedoms in accordance with their international obligations and national legislations.

The Contracting Parties in accordance with their international obligations as well as national legislations, shall guarantee in their territories the observance of legitimate rights and interests of citizens of the other Contracting Parties residing in their territories, and shall facilitate the provision of necessary mutual legal assistance.

Article 12

The Contracting Parties shall recognize and protect each other's legitimate rights and interests relative to the property possessed by a Contracting Party in the territory of another Contracting Party.

Article 13

The Contracting Parties shall strengthen economic cooperation on the basis of equality and mutual benefit and shall create favourable conditions for developing trade, encouraging investments and exchanging technologies within the framework of the SCO.

The Contracting Parties shall facilitate economic activities including the provision of legal conditions for activities, in their territories, of natural and legal persons of other Contracting Parties, who are engaged in a legal economic activity, as well as the protection in their territory of legitimate rights and interests of such natural and legal persons.

Article 14

The Contracting Parties shall develop cooperation in international financial institutions, economic organizations and fora, of which they are members, and shall facilitate membership of other Contracting Parties in those organizations in accordance with the statutory provisions of such institutions, organizations and fora.

Article 15

The Contracting Parties shall develop cooperation in the sphere of industry, agriculture, finance, energy, transport, science and technology, innovation, information, telecommunications, air space, and other spheres of mutual interest to them and shall encourage various forms of regional projects.

Article 16

The Contracting Parties shall take all possible measures to promote cooperation in the legal sphere; hold regular exchanges of information on the legislation under development, adopted or in force; and cooperate in the development of international legal instruments.

The Contracting Parties shall encourage contacts and cooperation between their legislative authorities and their representatives.

Article 17

The Contracting Parties shall develop cooperation in providing environmental protection, ecological security and sound environmental management and shall take necessary measures to develop and implement special programs and projects in these fields.

Article 18

The Contracting Parties shall render mutual support and assistance in preventing natural and technogenic emergencies and mitigating consequences thereof.

Article 19

The Contracting Parties shall develop mutual exchanges and cooperation in the fields of culture, art, education, science, technologies, health, tourism, sport and other social and humanitarian spheres.

The Contracting Parties shall mutually promote and support direct links between cultural, educational, scientific and research institutions; joint scientific and research programs and projects; as well as cooperation in training, exchange of students, scientists and specialists.

The Contracting Parties shall actively contribute to creating favourable conditions for studying the languages and cultures of other Contracting Parties.

Article 20

This Treaty shall not affect the rights and obligations of the Contracting Parties under other international treaties to which they are parties.

Article 21

To implement this Treaty, the Contracting Parties may conclude international agreements in specific fields of mutual interest.

Article 22

Disputes related to the interpretation or implementation of the provisions of this Treaty shall be settled through consultations and negotiations between the Contracting Parties.

Article 23

This Treaty shall be subject to ratification by the Contracting Parties—Signatories to it.

This Treaty shall be indefinite and shall enter into force from the date of deposit of the last instrument of ratification to the Depositary.

This Treaty shall remain in force for any Contracting Party while it is a Member State of the Organization. Participation of a Contracting Party in this Treaty shall cease automatically from the date of the termination of its membership in the SCO.

Upon entry into force of this Treaty, it shall be open for accession by any State that has become a member of the Organization. For the accessing State this Treaty shall enter into force on the thirtieth day from the date of deposit of the relevant instrument of accession to the Depositary.

Article 24

This Treaty may be amended and supplemented by separate protocols as agreed upon by all the Contracting Parties.

Article 25

The original copy of this Treaty shall be deposited with the Depositary.

The Secretariat of the Shanghai Cooperation Organization shall be the Depositary of this Treaty and shall transmit to the Contracting Parties certified copies thereof within fifteen days from the date of its signature.

Article 26

This Treaty shall be subject to registration with the United Nations Secretariat in accordance with Article 102 of the UN Charter.

Done in the city of Bishkek on 16 August 2007 in one copy in the Russian and Chinese languages, both texts being equally authentic.

Appendix XI

Dushanbe Declaration of the Heads of the Member States of the Shanghai Cooperation Organisation

The heads of the member states of the Shanghai Cooperation Organisation (hereinafter referred to as the SCO or the Organisation) having gathered in Dushanbe at the Heads of State Council meeting and having discussed issues of international and regional situation state the following:

1. In the 21st century interdependence of states has grown sharply, security and development are becoming inseparable. None of the modern international problems can be settled by force, the role of force factor in global and regional politics is diminishing objectively.

Reliance on a solution based solely on the use of force faces no prospects, it hinders comprehensive settlement of local conflicts; effective resolution of existing problems can be possible only with due regard for the interests of all parties, through their involvement in a process of negotiations, not through isolation. Attempts to strengthen one's own security to the prejudice of security of others do not assist the maintenance of global security and stability.

The participants of the Dushanbe meeting underline the need to respect historical and cultural traditions of every state and the efforts aimed to preserve unity and territorial integrity of states as well as to encourage good-neighbourly relations among peoples and their common development.

2. Search for effective response to common challenges and threats that are global in nature must be conducted in strict accordance with the UN Charter and generally accepted norms of the international law, by uniting the efforts of all states, overcoming the bloc mentality, bloc politics and unipolarity, using the means of multilateral diplomacy.

The member states of the SCO believe that in modern circumstances the international security must be built on the principles of mutual trust, mutual benefit, equality and cooperation. The creation of a global antimissile defence system does not assist the maintenance of strategic balance, international efforts on weapons control and nuclear non-proliferation, strengthening of trust among states and regional stability.

3. The member states of the SCO express their deep concern in connection with the recent tension around the issue of South Ossetia, and call on the relevant parties to resolve existing problems in a peaceful way through dialogue, to make efforts for reconciliation and facilitation of negotiations.

The member states of the SCO welcome the signing on 13 August 2008 in Moscow of the six principles of settling the conflict in South Ossetia, and support the active role of Russia in promoting peace and cooperation in the region.

4. The member states of the SCO reaffirm their commitment to preventive diplomacy as an important tool for effective settlement of the problems of security protection and development, as well as to strengthening the key role of the UN in the field of crisis prevention.

The member states of the SCO proceed from the assumption that articles of the UN Charter, resolutions of the Security Council and norms of the international law serve as the legitimate base for conflict prevention, and the UN SC whose main responsibility lies in maintaining international peace and security is to play a defining role in this field.

Noting the increasingly active role and growing potential of regional organisations in the field of preventive diplomacy the member states of the SCO stand up for comprehensive development and enhancement of cooperation between the UN and regional bodies in accordance with Chapter VIII of the UN Charter.

5. The member states of the Organisation stand up for broad international collaboration in resolving the problem of resources supply to satisfy the needs of mankind without damaging the environment, in achieving the goals of global development, e.g. closing the technological gap among states and elimination of poverty by providing all states equal access to the advantages of globalisation.

Against the backdrop of a slowdown in the growth of world economy pursuing a responsible currency and financial policy, control over the capital movement, ensuring food and energy security have been gaining special significance.

6. The member states of the SCO express satisfaction at the increased interaction in fighting terrorism, separatism and extremism in the framework of the Organisation, and intend to raise cooperation of the member states in the field of ensuring security to a qualitatively

new level by using the means of the Regional Antiterrorist Structure of the SCO.

The member states of the SCO reaffirm their commitment to strengthening the central coordinating role of the UN in mounting an international response to the threat of terrorism, to consistent implementation of the Global Counterterrorism Strategy, earliest possible approval of the Comprehensive Convention on International Terrorism.

The member states of the SCO are determined to counter the attempts of spreading terrorist ideology, stand ready to interact closely in implementing Resolution 1624 of the UN SC, as well as in promoting dialogue among civilisations and cultures. In this battle it is also essential to rely on the potential of civil society, business circles, mass media and non-governmental organisations.

7. The heads of state stress the importance of the adoption at the 62nd session of the UN General Assembly of Resolution 62/17 "Developments in the field of information and telecommunications in the context of international security" and express their readiness to jointly assist the fulfillment of its recommendations.

The heads of state note the fruitful work under the auspices of the SCO on creating international legal framework and practical mechanisms of cooperation in the field of ensuring international information security.

8. The heads of state stand up for deepening interaction between the SCO and the United Nations Organisation, as well as the Commonwealth of Independent States, Association of Southeast Asian Nations, Eurasian Economic Community, Collective Security Treaty Organisation, Economic Cooperation Organisation and the United Nations Economic and Social Commission for Asia and the Pacific on the basis of the signed memoranda of understanding.

9. The heads of state underline the importance of developing dialogue among the member states of the Organisation over issues of effective and rational use of water and energy resources with due regard for the interests of parties.

Bringing together the efforts to set up close cooperation in industrial exploration of new energy technologies, e.g. in the context of fighting the global climate change, will assume special significance. In this regard greater emphasis will be put on the formulation of common approaches of the SCO member states towards overcoming negative consequences of the climate change and developing eco-friendly sources of energy.

10. The member states of the SCO reaffirming their commitment to basic documents and standards in the field of protection and encouragement of human rights:

- promote the observance of basic human rights and civil liberties in accordance with international obligations and national legislation;
- share experience in enforcing international treaties on human rights;
- implement existing agreements in the framework of multilateral and bilateral treaties in the field of social and cultural cooperation;
- launch active consultations and cooperation at the UN on human rights issues;
- maintain interaction of the SCO with other regional organisations and integration-oriented associations on issues of social and cultural cooperation and human rights encouragement.

11. The member states of the SCO state that the geopolitical and economic significance of Central Asia keeps growing. The dynamic evolution of the Organisation will contribute to strengthening the strategic stability, maintaining peace and security, establishing multifaceted economic, social and cultural interaction in the region.

12. External challenges and security threats are the factor which complicates the situation in the region. Current developments in Afghanistan, increasing volumes of drugs trafficking, transnational organised crime determine the need to step up interaction, among others by creating joint mechanisms of assessment, prevention and response to such challenges and threats.

The heads of state consider it important that the International Security Assistance Force (ISAF) operating in Afghanistan on the mandate of the UN Security Council pay greater attention to the task of battling the production and trafficking of the Afghan narcotics in interaction with the government of the Islamic Republic of Afghanistan, neighbouring and other interested countries. They suggest outlining this task in the mandate of the ISAF during a regular discussion at the UN SC of the situation in Afghanistan.

The member states of the SCO will continue to make joint efforts to set up close interaction with other interested states, international regional organisations with the aim of creating a wide partnership network on counteraction against the threats of terrorism and narcotics.

The heads of state underline the need to increase the activity of the SCO-Afghanistan Contact Group as part of the efforts concerning interaction with Afghanistan, to launch practical preparations for convening a special conference on Afghanistan under the auspices of the SCO to discuss issues of joint counteraction against terrorism, illegal circulation of narcotics and organised crime.

13. The heads of state believe that the creation of a nuclear free zone in Central Asia is an important step aimed to consolidate the regime of the Treaty on the Non-Proliferation of Nuclear Weapons. In this regard they proceed from the assumption that the Semipalatinsk Treaty of 2006 will contribute to strengthening peace and security in the region and the fight against international nuclear terrorism by preventing nuclear materials and technologies from falling into the hands of non-state actors.

14. The Shanghai Cooperation Organisation is open for constructive dialogue with all international and regional organisations who share the objectives and principles of the SCO and conduct their activity in accordance with norms of the international law and the UN Charter. Proceeding from that the SCO stands ready to consider a possibility of establishing interaction with other international organisations with the aim of ensuring a stable, secure and harmonious development of the region with due regard and the fullest consideration for the interests of the SCO member states.

President of the Republic of Kazakhstan
Chairman of the People's Republic of China
President of the Kyrgyz Republic
President of the Russian Federation
President of the Republic of Tajikistan
President of the Republic of Uzbekistan

Appendix XII

Statement by the Shanghai Cooperation Organization Member States and the Islamic Republic of Afghanistan on Combating Terrorism, Illicit drug Trafficking and Organized Crime

The Member States of the Shanghai Cooperation Organization (SCO) and the Islamic Republic of Afghanistan,

Supporting the efforts of the Afghan Government, with the assistance of the international community, aimed at ensuring social and economic development, building democratic institutions, strengthening operational capability of the Afghan national army and police and enhancing the effectiveness of law enforcement bodies,

Recognizing the interconnected challenges facing Afghanistan, including continued terrorist activities and the cultivation, production and trafficking of narcotic drugs, and that both pose a serious threat the stability of Afghanistan, its neighbours and other countries,

While welcoming efforts of the Afghan Government to decrease cultivation of opium, express concern about the continued cultivation and production of narcotics drugs as a source of financing terrorist activities in Afghanistan, the region and abroad,

Supporting the efforts of the Afghan Government and International Security Assistance Force in Afghanistan (ISAF) to improve law enforcement and combat the production and trafficking of narcotic drugs and curtailing the flow of precursors more effectively,

Noting the significant assistance provided by the SCO Member States to the Afghan Government and their commitment to sustain such support for tackling the challenges in Afghanistan,

Stressing the importance of maintaining the leading role of the United Nations in coordinating international assistance in Afghanistan,

Attaching great importance to the efforts made by international and regional organizations including the United Nations (UN), the Shanghai Cooperation Organization (SCO), the Commonwealth of Independent States (CIS), the Collective Security Treaty Organization

(CSTO), the Organization for Security and Cooperation in Europe (OSCE) and Conference on Interaction and Confidence Building Measures in Asia (CICA) to combat the threats of terrorism, illicit drug trafficking and organized crime,

Declare the following:

1. Combating Illicit Drug Trafficking

We call upon all States concerned to implement, in the framework of the United Nations activities, and other international and regional organizations, existing international strategies to combat narcotics in Afghanistan and the region, which in particular provide for strict implementation of Resolution 1817 of the UN Security Council and decisions of relevant international fora, as well as for creating and reinforcing the "anti-drug and financial security belts" in the region.

We call for further improvement of the SCO drug control cooperation mechanism as well as the elaboration of plans of practical cooperation between anti-drug agencies of the SCO Member States and other states of the region, including information exchange, precursor control and close interaction between this mechanism and relevant UN agencies, as well as other international and regional organizations involved in combating cultivation, production and trafficking of narcotics.

We stress the need to strengthen international and regional cooperation to counter the threat of narcotics, including through support of programs and projects implemented by the UN, the CSTO, the CIS, the EU, and the OSCE in Afghanistan and Central Asia related to border security and management.

We call for joining the efforts of all States and organizations concerned aimed at creating the "anti-drug and financial security belts" in the region.

We welcome the fact that ISAF in cooperation with the Government of Afghanistan joined the fight against drug production and proliferation in Afghanistan and support its wide-ranging participation in multilateral efforts in this area. We consider it important that the UN Security Council takes this into account when discussing the ISAF mandate next time.

We call for wider cooperation between the SCO, CSTO and CIS on the anti-drug and counter-terrorism tracks, and stress the importance of the multilateral preventive operation named Operation

Channel carried out under the CSTO auspices, as well as of increasing the number of observer States participating in this operation.

We believe that full operationalization of the Central Asia Regional Information and Coordination Centre established to combat illicit trafficking in narcotic drugs, psychotropic substances and their precursors with the participation of Afghanistan will strengthen control over the illicit production and abuse of and trafficking in narcotic drugs, psychotropic substances and precursors in Central Asia.

2. Combating International Terrorism

We believe that the list of priorities for the international community in combating terrorism should include the improvement of its international legal framework, in particular early elaboration and adoption of a comprehensive convention on international terrorism as well as the elaboration of regional counter-terrorism legal instruments.

We call for adherence to relevant resolutions of the UN Security Council concerning international terrorism.

We call for stopping the attempts to spread terrorist ideology as well as for strict compliances with UN SC Resolution 1624 (2005), which condemns all acts of terrorism irrespective of their motivation, and call upon Member States to prohibit by law terrorist acts and incitement to commit such acts, as well as to deny safe heaven to those guilty of committing these acts; and we consider it important to advance international, inter-ethnic and inter-religious dialogue in order to fight terrorist ideology, which would involve the civil society, including religious leaders, mass media, business communities and educational structures.

We reaffirm our intention to continue participating in the activities of the Financial Action Task Force (FATF) and the Eurasian Group on combating Money-Laundering and Financing of Terrorism (EAG), in particular with a view to stop the financial flows related to illicit trafficking in drugs and their precursors, and to make it a separate area in the EAG and FATF activities.

The SCO Member States intend to invest more efforts in combating terrorist threat using the capacity of the SCO Regional Anti-Terrorism Structure to a greater extent, and the practice of joint SCO counter-terrorism exercises, and we invite Observer States and other countries concerned to participate in the collective efforts, including those related to creating the "anti-terrorist security belt", and consider taking part in transiting non-military cargoes needed by ISAF.

The SCO Member States with the assistance of the Afghan Government will advance cooperation in responding to terrorist threats, ensuring security and protection of their citizens and diplomatic missions in Afghanistan.

3. Combating Transnational Organized Crime

We reaffirm our firm commitment to counter the growing illegal trafficking in arms, munitions, explosive and other types of transnational organized crime, which pose a serious threat to the lives and security of our peoples.

We believe that an effective coordination mechanism for the competent authorities to be established within the SCO in the form of meetings between the ministers of interior affairs and public security, as well as fostering and developing links with competent authorities of other States, international and regional agencies will help in combating organized crime.

× × ×

We believe that a regular dialogue on joint action against abovementioned threats to be launched within the SCO with participations of other States and international organizations concerned could become an effective supplement to the existing international fora for addressing the challenges of terrorism, narcotics and organized crime in the region.

We express our commitment to enhance cooperation with all relevant States and international and regional organizations, namely UN, EU, CIS, CSTO, OSCE, NATO and CICA on matters of common interest in the spirit of this Statement and the Plan of Action of the Shanghai Cooperation Organization Member States and the Islamic Republic of Afghanistan on combating terrorism, illicit drug trafficking and organized crime.

Appendix XIII

Yekaterinburg Declaration of the Heads of the Member States of the Shanghai Cooperation Organisation

In accordance with the outcome of the Heads of State Council meeting held on 15 and 16 June 2009 in Yekaterinburg the heads of the member states of the Shanghai Cooperation Organisation state the following:

1. Serious changes are taking place in the contemporary international environment. Aspiration to peace and sustainable development, promotion of equal cooperation became the spirit of the times. The tendency towards true multipolarity is irreversible. There is a growing significance of the regional aspect in settling global problems.

The SCO member states, reaffirming their commitment to common development on the basis of the principles and provisions of the Charter of the Shanghai Cooperation Organisation and the Treaty on Long-Term Good-Neighbourly Relations, Friendship and Cooperation among the SCO Member States, consider as a priority task maintaining constructive dialogue and deepening close interaction and partnership to jointly seek effective ways of resolving global and regional problems with the use of the growing potential and international prestige of the SCO.

2. The SCO member states believe that international cooperation is a basic and efficient instrument for countering new challenges and threats, coping with the global financial crisis, ensuring energy and food security and settling such a pressing issue as climate change.

3. The current situation in the global economic and financial sector points to the need to increase cooperation of the international community in the field of controlling and managing international finances, making joint efforts to prevent the growth and spread of financial crisis risks, maintaining economic stability.

The member states of the Organisation together with the international community intend to make efforts for the formation of a more just, equal, all-embracing and well-regulated international financial regime which takes into account a true balance of interests of all its participants and gives all States equal access to the advantages of globalisation.

To that end interaction and sharing of information must be strengthened as regards the international financial sector and the issues of tackling the consequences of the global financial crisis in the SCO region.

4. In current circumstances the SCO member states underline the growing significance of bolstering trade, economic and investment cooperation in the framework of the Organisation, including involving the potential of the observer states and dialogue partners.

The parties noted the need to speed up the implementation of major projects which are designed to ensure the expansion of transport communication capabilities of the region and access to world markets, development of social infrastructure, formation of modern international centres for logistics, trade and tourism, construction of new factories, introduction of innovative and energy-saving technologies, including renewable sources of energy.

The implementation of these projects, arrangement of international transport corridors, modernisation of railways and motorways will create preconditions for strengthening the potential of the region as a transcontinental bridge and giving a new impulse to the development of economic links between Europe and Asia.

5. The SCO member states, noting the key significance of energy sector for successful economic development and creation of favourable preconditions for improving the living standards of their citizens, express determination to further advance mutually beneficial cooperation in this field on the basis of equality with the aim of ensuring effective, reliable and environmentally safe energy supplies.

6. The Shanghai Cooperation Organisation proceeds from the need to further cement the legal foundations of international relations determined by generally accepted principles and norms of the international law and international obligations of States.

Strengthening the central and coordinating role of the United Nations Organisation in world affairs, enhancing the effectiveness of its mechanisms with the aim of adequately responding to modern challenges, changing political and economic reality remains an urgent task. The reform of the UN Security Council must gain as much wider consensus of members of the international community.

The SCO member states intend to strengthen coordination on the issues of reforming the UN and its Security Council.

7. The SCO member states stress the significance of the issue of

ensuring international information security as one of the key elements of the common system of international security.

8. The SCO member states, reaffirming their commitment to a dialogue of civilisations, values of peace, tolerance, mutual respect and consent in international and interdenominational relations, irrespective of ethnic origin, religious and other beliefs, oppose drawing parallels between the fight against international terrorism and confrontation against any particular religion.

9. Maintenance of international peace is possible only in conditions of equal security for all States. The security of some states must not be achieved to the detriment of the security of others.

Settlement of international and regional conflicts must be conducted by political diplomatic means on the basis of the principles of equality and mutual respect, non-interference in internal affairs of sovereign states.

The attempts to achieve unilateral advantages in defence field are counterproductive as they undermine the strategic balance and stability in the world, do not benefit confidence building, reduction of arms and disarmament.

10. The SCO member states note that proliferation of nuclear weapons poses a serious threat to international peace and security.

The Treaty on the Non-Proliferation of Nuclear Weapons (NNPT) is the basic element of the international regime on the prevention of proliferation of nuclear weapons. Threats of proliferation of nuclear weapons can and must be eliminated on the basis of the NNPT provided that its parties unconditionally fulfill their obligations. The SCO member states reaffirm their strong support for the NNPT, welcome the multilateral efforts on its reinforcement, and are determined to move towards raising the effectiveness of the Treaty on the basis of the unity of its three key components: non-proliferation, disarmament, peaceful use of nuclear energy.

The SCO member states reiterate their intention to assist further implementation of the Russia—U.S. initiative on fighting against acts of nuclear terrorism, and also welcome the coming into effect on 21 March 2009 of the Treaty on Establishing a Nuclear Free Zone in Central Asia.

11. The SCO member states welcome the start of Russo-American negotiations on drafting a Treaty on the Reduction of Offensive Strategic Arms.

12. The SCO member states stand up for resuming the process of negotiations on the denuclearisation of the Korean peninsula. They call to show restraint and continue the search for mutually acceptable solutions on the basis of the previously reached agreements.

13. The SCO member states express grave concern over the complicated situation in Afghanistan related to illicit drug trafficking, terrorism and transnational organised crime which pose a threat to the whole international community.

In this regard the parties acknowledged the need to increase interaction with the SCO observer states, Afghanistan and other states concerned, as well as with regional and international organisations, first and foremost, the UN and its specialised institutions.

The SCO member states in close interaction with other states and international organisations concerned intend to establish anti-narcotic and financial security belts in the region.

14. The SCO member states welcome the end of an internal military conflict in Sri Lanka, and express hope for establishing a firm peace, strengthening security and stability in the country on the basis of ensuring its state sovereignty and territorial integrity, guaranteeing the rights of all ethnic and religious groups.

15. The SCO member states consider as a priority task enhancing the effectiveness of interaction in the field of a timely joint response to natural and manmade emergency events, implementing a set of measures aimed to diminish their impact on society and economy.

16. The SCO member states attach special importance to strengthening cooperation in the field of effective counteraction against the threat of dangerous infections and other infectious diseases. To that end the parties acknowledged the need to mobilise available resources and launch joint work on preventing the spread of epidemic diseases.

17. The SCO member countries state that the Organisation has become an essential element of the fledgling system of security and cooperation in the Asia Pacific region.

Noting with satisfaction the growing interest of the international community in establishing ties with the SCO, they welcome the joining of the Republic of Belarus and the Democratic Socialist Republic of Sri Lanka to cooperation in the SCO framework as dialogue partners.

The SCO member states stand ready to expand practical interaction with the United Nations Organisation, Commonwealth of Independent States, Association of South-East Asian Nations, Eurasian Economic Community, Collective Security Treaty Organisation, Economic Cooperation Organisation, United Nations Economic and Social Commission for Asia and the Pacific, other international and regional organisations, and to create on this basis a wide partnership network.

The SCO member states are open to dialogue aimed to bring States closer together and facilitate the building of a more just world order, to cement global stability and economic development.

President of the Republic of Kazakhstan
Chairman of the People's Republic of China
President of the Kyrgyz Republic
President of the Russian Federation
President of the Republic of Tajikistan
President of the Republic of Uzbekistan

Yekaterinburg, 16 June 2009

Bibliography

Documents

Shanghai Convention on Combating Terrorism, Separatism and Extremism, 2001

Declaration on Establishment of Shanghai Cooperation Organisation, 2001

Charter of Shanghai Cooperation Organisation, 2002

Provisional Scheme for Mutual Relations between Shanghai Cooperation Organisation and Other International Organisations and States, Moscow 23 November 2002

Moscow Declaration of Heads of Member States of Shanghai Cooperation Organisation, 2003

Declaration of Heads of Member States of Shanghai Cooperation Organisation, Tashkent, 2004

Joint Communiqué of the Meeting of the Council of Heads of Member States of the Shanghai Cooperation Organisation, 2005

Joint Communiqué of the Meeting of the Council of Heads of Member States of the Shanghai Cooperation Organisation, Shanghai, 2006

Bishkek Declaration of the Heads of the Member States of the Shanghai Cooperation Organisation, 2007

Treaty on Long-Term Good-Neighbourliness, Friendship and Cooperation Between member States of the Shanghai Cooperation Organisation, Bishkek, 2007

SCO Summit Meeting issues Joint Communiqué, Bishkek, 2007

Joint Communiqué of the Meeting of Council of the Heads of the Member States of the Shanghai Cooperation Organisation, (Dushanbe); 2008.

Dushanbe Declaration of the Heads of the Member States of the Shanghai Cooperation Organisation, 2008.

SCO Leaders issue Joint-Declaration on Security, Energy, 2008

Statement by the Shanghai Cooperation Organisation Member States and the Islamic Republic of Afghanistan on Combating Terrorism, Illicit Drug Trafficking and Organised Crime, Moscow, March 2009

Yekaterinburg Declaration of the Heads of the Member States of the Shanghai Cooperation Organisation, 2009

Joint Communiqué of the Meeting of Council of the Heads of the Member States of the Shanghai Cooperation Organisation, 2009

Books and Articles

Agence France Presse, "Putin Takes Swipe at US Policy in Central Asia", June 15, 2006, archive.turkishpress.com/news.asp?id=128802.

Akatayeva, Aliya, "Security Issues in Central Asia and the Shanghai Cooperation Organization" *Contemporary Central Asia*, Vol. 9, No. 2-3, Aug-Dec, 2005, pp. 81-83.

Alexander Lukin, *Russia's Image of China and Russian-Chinese Relations*, MGIMO, Moscow, 2002.

Alexander Lukin, "Shanghaiskakya Organizatsiya: Sotrudnichesto, Strukturnaya Oformlenia i Perspektivy Razvitiya", *Analyticheskie Zapiski*, vyp. 2(4) February 2005.

Ambrosio, Thomas, "Catching the 'Shanghai spirit': How the Shanghai Cooperation Organization promotes authoritarian norms in Central Asia", *Europe-Asia Studies*, Vol. 60, No. 8, Oct, 2008, pp. 1321-44.

Anand Vinod, "Shanghai Cooperation Organization: Problems and Prospects", *USI Journal*, Vol. 137, No. 569, July-Sep, 2007, pp. 369-77.

Aris, Stephen, "The Shanghai Cooperation Organisation: 'Tackling the three evil'. A regional response to non-traditional security challenges or an anti-Western bloc?" *Europe-Asia Studies*, Vol. 61, No. 3, May 2009, pp. 457-82.

Brummer, Matthew, "Shanghai Cooperation Organization and Iran: A powerfull union", *Journal of International Affairs*, Vol. 60, No. 2, Spring-Summer 2007, pp. 185-98.

Chung, Chien-Peng, "Shanghai Cooperation Organization: China's changing influence in Central Asia", *China Quarterly*, No. 180, Dec. 2004, p. 989-1109.

Devendra Kaushik, "Building a New Security System through Regional Cooperation: Renewal of Bandung Spirit', in Mahavir Singh (ed.) *Building a New Asia*, Delhi, 2005.

Devendra Kaushik, "India-Russia-China, Triangle to Transform the Present World Order", in Mahavir Singh (ed.), *Asia Annual*, 2004, Shipra, New Delhi, 2005

Dietl, Gulshan, "SCO: a checkmate on a chessboard", *Contemporary Central Asia*, Vol. 11, No. 1-3, Apr-Dec, 2007, pp. 5-29.

Dina R. Spechler and Martin C. Spechler, "Trade, Energy, and Security in the Central Asian Arena", in Ashley J. Tellis and Michael Wills, eds., *Strategic Asia 2006-07: Trade, Interdependence, and Security, Seattle, WA: 2006, p. 225.*

Dingi Shen, "China's Energy Problem and Alternative Solution", *Journal of Contemporary China*, Vol. 10, No. 29, 2001.

Dmitri Kosyrev, "China's Shadow over the Moskva" *Pioneer*, 21 September 2006.

Dmitri Kosyrev, "Engaging with Friend and brother" *Pioneer*, 21 March 2006.

Dmitri Kosyrev, "Rush Demand for Shanghai Cooperation Organization", *RIA Novosti*, August 17, 2007.

Dmitri K. Simes, *After the Collapse: Russia Seeks its Place as a Great Power*, New York, Simon and Schuster, 1999.

Dmitri Trenin, "Russia and the Shanghai Cooperation Organisation: A Difficult Match", *CEF Quarterly: The Journal of the China-Eurasia Forum*, July 2005, p. 26.

Dmitri Trenin, *The End of Eurasia: Russia on the Border between Geopolitics and Globalization*, Washington, D.C.: Carnegie Endowment for International Peace, 2002.

German Gref, "Russian-Chinese Relations: On Right Track", *RIA Novosti*, September 11, 2006.

Gilbert Rozman, *A Mirror for Socialism: Soviet Criticism of China*, Princeton University Press, Princeton, 1985.

Girijesh Pant, "American Energy Policy in the Caspian Region: The Changing Energy Security Dynamics" (Unpublished project Paper)

Gleason, Gregory, "Inter-state cooperation in Central Asia from the CIS to the Shanghai forum", *Europe-Asia Studies*, Vol. 53, No. 7, Nov. 2001, pp. 1077-95.

Howe, Christopher, "Shanghai in the long run", *China Quarterly*, No. 184, Dec. 2005, pp. 952-58.

Huasheng, Zhao, "Shanghai Cooperation Organization: An overview of Security and Economic Cooperation", *World Affairs*, Vol. 10, No. 3, Autumn 2006, pp. 128-40.

Igor Tomberg, "Energy Outcome of SCO Meeting in Dushanbe", September 20, 2006, en.rian,ru/analysis/20060920/54104304.shtml.

"Isolation of Russian Far East Threat to National Security—Putin", *RIA Novosti*, December 20, 2006, en.rian.ru/Russia/20061220/57396954.html.

James Brooke, "Russia's Far East hopes to Power China", *International Herald Tribune*, 24 March 2004.

Kabir, Mahfuz, "Expansion of Shanghai Cooperation Organisation: Iran's horizons and perspectives", *Biiss Journal*, Vol. 27, No. 3, July 2006, pp. 250-70.

Khalid Mahmud, "Shanghai Cooperation Organisation (SCO): Beginning of a new partnership", *Regional Studies*, Vol. 20, No. 1, Winter, 2001-202, p. 3-18.

Kozhokin, Yevgeny: Shanghai Five: Present realities and Future Prospects", *Strategic Digest*, Vol. 21, No. 7, July 2001, pp. 883-90.

Kumar, Raman, "Shanghai Five: A Profile", JNU M.Phil Thesis.

Lanteigne, Marc, "In medias res: the development of the Shanghai Cooperation Organization as a Security Community" *Pacific Affairs*, Vol. 79, No. 4, Winter 2007, pp. 605-22.

Li Jingjie, "Pillars of Sino-Russian Partnership", *Orbis*, Fall, 2000.

Lowell Dittmer, *Sino-Soviet Normalization and its International Implications, 1945-1990*, Seattle, University of Washington Press.

Luzyanin, Sergey, "Central Asia in trilateral cooperation; regional potential and resources of SCO", *China Report*, Vol. 43, No. 2, Apr-June, 2007, pp. 237-43.

Ma Jiali, "Central Asia: Geo-Strategic Situation and Big Powers' Policies", *Contemporary Central Asia*, Vol. III, No. 1, 1999.

Mohanty, A.K., "Russian understanding of China's SCO Policy", *China Report*, Vol. 43, No. 2, Apr-June, 2007, pp. 245-57.

Nicklas Norling and Niklas Swanström, "Sino-Russian Relations in Central Asia and the SCO", CACI Analyst, October 3, 2007.

Norling, Nicklas, "Shanghai Cooperation Organization, trade, and the roles of Iran, India and Pakistan", *Central Asian Survey*, Vol. 26, No. 3, Sep, 2007, pp. 429-44.

Pallavi Aiyar, "More than Neighbours, Less Than Friends?" *The Hindu*, March 26, 2007.

"President Hu Jinto Holds Talks with His Russian Counterpart Putin", Ministry of Foreign Affairs of the People's Republic of China, March 27, 2007, www.fmprc.gov.cn/eng/zxxx/t306902.htm.

Qinhua, Xu, "SCO and Russia-China-India triangular relations", *Himalayan and Central Asian Studies*, Vol. 12, No. 2, Apr-June 2008.

Roy, Ash Narain, "Shanghai Cooperation Organization: Towards new dydnamism" *Mainstream*, Vol. 45, No. 39, 15 Sep. 2007, pp. 31-32.

Russian scholars on "Shanghai Cooperation Organisation (SCO), International situation of China", *Mainstream*, Vol. 46, No. 1, 15 Nov. 2008, pp. 8-9.

Sahai, Kajari, "Declaration of the Shanghai Cooperation Organisation", *China Report*, Vol. 38, No. 1, Jan-Mar., 2002, pp. 129-32.

Sbornik Rossiisko-Kitaiskikh dogovorov, 1949-1999, Moscow, 1999.

SCO Could admit new members in June—Official—*RIA-NOVOSTI,* 13.04.2006

Stephen J. Blank and Alvin Z. Rubenstine (ed.) *Imperial Decline: Russia's Changing Role in Asia*, Duke University Press, Durham 1997.

Stobdan, P., "Shanghai Treaty: Reading the frontiers", *Strategic Analysis*, vol. 19, No. 3, June 96, pp. 513-20.

Sunanda K. Datta Ray, "Can a New Trio Shoulder America's burden in Asia", *International Herald Tribune*, 25 June 2005.

Swaran Singh, "India and the Shanghai Forum", *Strategic Analysis*, Vol. 24 No. 6, Sep. 2000, pp. 171-76.

"Trade, Economic Cooperation Priorities for Russia, China—Putin", *Ria Novosti*, March 26, 2007, en.rian.ru/Russia/20070326/62647755.html.

Viktor Litovkin, "SCO Military Task" *Ria-Novosti*, 11.05.2006.

V. Gel'bras, *Aziatsko-Tikhookeanskiy Region: Problelmy Ekonomicheskoi Bezopasnosti Rossii*, Moscow, 1995.

Viktor Litovkin, "Sino-Russian Exercise" Thwarting Separatist and Terrorist Operations" *The Statesman*, 28 May 2005.

Vladimir Radyuhin, "More than just neighbours", *The Hindu*, 29 August 2005.

Wadlow, Rene, "Shanghai Cooperation Organization: A Balance of Opportunity", *World Affairs*, Vol. 10, No. 2, Summer 2006, pp. 57-71.

Wall, David, "Shanghai Cooperation Organization: Five candles, three evils", *World Today*, Vol. 62, No. 6, June 2006, pp. 20-21.

Watson, N.J., "Central Asia: More than a talking shop, just", *Petroleum Economist*, Vol. 74, No. 10, Oct. 2007, p. 30.

Wu, Junfei, "Will SCO become another Warsaw Pact", *Economic and Political Weekly*, Vol. 40 No. 39, 24-30 Sep. 2005, pp. 4205-07.

Y. Bazanov, "Big Neighbour—Big Headaches", *New Times*, August 1996.

Yu Bin, "China-Russia Relations: Pollution, Politics, and Partnership", *Comparative Connections*, Vol. 7, No. 4, January 2006, pp. 135-136.

Zhao Huaheng, "China, Russia, and the United States: Prospects or Cooperation in Central Asia", *CEF Quarterly: The Journal of the China-Eurasia Forum*, February 2005, p. 24.

Zharmukhamed Zardykhan, "Kazakhstan and Central Asia: Regional Perspective", *Central Asian Survey*, Vol. 21, No. 2, 2002.

Zhuangzhi, Sun, "New and Old Regionalism: The Shanghai Cooperation Organisation and Sino-Central Asian relations", *Review of International Affairs*, Vol. 3 No. 4, Summer, 2004, p. 600-12.

Z. Khallilzade, etc., *The United States and a Rising China: Strategic and Military Implications, RAND, 1999.*

Index